C000101712

Hg2 Stockholm

A Hedonist's guide to
Stockholm

Written by Stephen Whitlock
Photographed by Ed Lane Fox

A HEDONIST'S GUIDE TO STOCKHOLM
2nd Edition

Managing director – Tremayne Carew Pole
Marketing director – Sara Townsend
Series editor – Catherine Blake
Design – Katy Platt
Maps – Richard Hale & Amber Sheers
Repro – Dorchester Typesetting
Printers – Printed in China by Leo
Publisher – Filmer Ltd

Additional photographs by Scarlett Stapleton, Tremayne Carew Pole,
Stephen Whitlock, Richard Ryan, Alexander Dokukin, Henrik Trygg
(Play), Johan Fouelin (Moderna Museet), Michele Masucci (Akki Sushi),
Graham Wong.

Email – info@hg2.com
Website – www.hg2.com

First published in the United Kingdom in May 2008 by
Filmer Ltd
47 Filmer Road,
London SW6 7JJ

ISBN – 978-1-905428-24-3

Hg2 Stockholm

CONTENTS

How to…

A Hedonist's guide to Stockholm is broken down into easy to use sections: Sleep, Eat, Drink, Snack, Party, Culture, Shop, Play, and Info. In each of these sections you will find detailed reviews and photographs. At the front of the book you will find an introduction to the city and an overview map, followed by introductions to the five main areas and more detailed maps. On each of these maps you will see the places that we have reviewed, laid out by section, highlighted on the map with a symbol and a number. To find out about a particular place simply turn to the relevant section, where all entries are listed alphabetically. Alternatively, browse through a specific section (e.g. Eat) until you find a restaurant that you like the look of. Next to your choice will be a coloured box – each colour refers to a particular area of the city. Simply turn to the relevant map to discover the location.

Updates

Hg2 have developed a network of journalists in each city to review the best hotels, restaurants, bars, clubs, etc., and to keep track of the latest developments – new places open up all the time, while others simply fade away or just go out of style. To access our free updates as well as the content of each guide, simply log onto our website www.Hg2.com and register. We welcome your help. If you have any comments or recommendations, please feel free to email us at info@hg2.com.

Book your hotel on Hg2.com

We believe that the key to a great city break is choosing the right hotel. Our unique site now enables you to browse through our selection of hotels, using the interactive maps to give you a good feel for the area as well as the nearby restaurants, bars, sights, etc., before you book. Hg2 has formed partnerships with the hotels featured in our guide to bring them to readers at the lowest possible price. Our site now incorporates special offers from selected hotels, as well as a diary of interesting events taking place, "Inspire Me."

The concept

A Hedonist's guide to... is designed to appeal to a more urbane and stylish traveler. The kind of traveler who is interested in gourmet food, elegant hotels and seriously chic bars – the traveler who feels the need to explore, shop, and pamper themselves away from the crowds.

Our aim is to give you an insider's knowledge of a city, to make you feel like a well-heeled, sophisticated local, and to take you to the most fashionable places in town to rub shoulders with the local glitterati.

In today's world work rules our life, and weekends away are few and far between; when we do manage to get away we want to have as much fun and to relax as much as possible with the minimum amount of stress. This guide is all about maximizing time. There is a photograph of each place we feature, so before you go you know exactly what you are getting into; choose a restaurant or bar that suits you and your needs.

We pride ourselves on our independence and our integrity. We eat in all the restaurants, drink in all the bars, and go wild in the nightclubs – all totally incognito. We charge no one for the privilege for appearing in the guide, and every place is reviewed and included at our discretion.

We feel cities are best enjoyed by soaking up the atmosphere: wander the streets, indulge in some retail therapy, re-energize yourself with a massage and then get ready to eat like a king and party hard on the local scene.

Stockholm

Abba got it right: Stockholm really is a 'Summer Night City'. The Swedish summer is usually wonderful and sometimes it's breathtaking.

In June, July and August the locals make the most of the warmer months, no doubt remembering how long and dark the winters can be. People seem to have boundless energy and spend much of their time sitting at outdoor cafés, swimming in the waters around Kungsholmen and Södermalm, sailing out into the archipelago and meeting up in the city's parks to drink box wine and cook sausages on little disposable grills that can be purchased from the supermarket.

In July the Swedes take their annual holiday. Many Stockholmers retreat to their country houses or set off on long sailing trips leaving the city extremely quiet, especially since some shops and restaurants close up for the month.

As summer eases into autumn, the city is no less spectacular. Expect days of high blue skies and cool, bright sunshine. This is the season for kicking through the leaves on a walk through Djurgården (see right), the island close to Östermalm that makes you feel as if you are in the middle of the Swedish countryside. With a bit of luck, September and October can be lovely.

But then comes November and the onset of winter. Or should we say winters? The Swedish winter seems more like three seasons than one. There's early winter, midwinter and late winter. Early winter, in November and the start of December, is dark and dank, with lots of mist and drizzle. Late winter, from late February to the start of April, is brighter but often wet and gloomy. But between them comes midwinter and it can be magical.

In the heart of a good Swedish winter, the water freezes around the islands and snow blankets the streets, which makes the dark days seem brighter. It's cold but usually not windy and the city adapts to make the most of the chill. Around Christmas, outdoor markets are set up with stalls selling *glögg* (warm mulled wine). Ice-skating rinks appear and children can ride up and down Kungsträdgården on Shetland ponies. Cafés and restaurants place burning candles outside their doors to show they are open.

So, if you are faced with the question of when to visit Stockholm, there are only two times to be wary of: early winter and late winter. Opt instead for summer, autumn or the not-so-bleak midwinter. Incidentally, spring hardly exists at all in Sweden. Late winter drags on forever until, over the course of one long weekend, the residents realise with a start that early summer has begun.

Whichever season you choose, bring shoes you can walk in. Stockholm is a small capital by world standards and it's possible to see most of the key sights in a couple of days, pausing for nice long lunches. In the summer, you should also plan on spending at least one day exploring the archipelago.

The city covers several islands, making it easy to divide into navigable areas. To help you plan your days, we've concentrated on the four districts that will prove most useful for a visitor to Stockholm: Gamla Stan, Norrmalm/Vasastan, Östermalm and Södermalm.

5

3

NORRMALM

VASASTADEN

13

17

9

1

KUNGSHOLMEN

14 **15** **10** **11**

7

8

GAMLA STAN

Riddarfjärden

LÅNGHOLMEN

SÖDERMALM

12

Liljeholmsviken

LILJEHOLMEN

Årstaviken

ÅRSTA

0   1 km

Stockholm city map

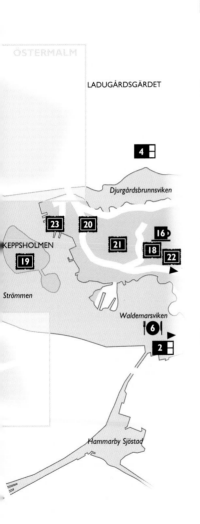

SLEEP

1. First Hotel Amaranten
2. Hotel J Nacka Strand
3. Stallmästaregarden
4. Villa Kallhagen

EAT

5. Edsbacka Krog
6. Fjäderholmarnas Krog
7. Kungsholmen
8. Lux

DRINK

9. Allmänna Galleriet
10. Kungsholmen
11. Lokal

SNACK

12. Lasse i Parken
13. Mellqvist
14. Muffin Bakery
15. Mälarpaviljongen
16. Rosendals Trädgård
17. Xoko

CULTURE

18. Djurgården
19. Moderna Museet
20. Nordiska Museet
21. Skansen
22. Thielska Galleriet
23. Vasamuséet

Gamla Stan

The obvious place to begin any visit to Stockholm is Gamla Stan, which is also known as the Old Town. This is the island in the centre of the city, which serves as a stepping stone from Norrmalm to the north and Södermalm to the south. There's much to love here, and also much to avoid.

The first thing to strike you is that Gamla Stan has charm in abundance. With its narrow cobbled streets flanked by ancient buildings in shades of sage green, mustard yellow and red, it's easily the most photographed part of town. There are lots of little alleyways just waiting to be explored, and you'll stumble across cafés (a few of them good) and places to stop for an ice-cream in the summer. Unfortunately also plentiful are the ghastly souvenir shops, selling T-shirts emblazoned with images of moose and slogans such as 'Take a liking to a Viking', no end of bad restaurants and hordes of tourists who clog the narrow arteries of the Old Town like packs of slow-witted elk.

The good news is that most of these problems can easily be avoided. For starters, avoid Västerlånggatan, the main tourist street, in favour of those running parallel with it. If you want to stay in the Old Town,

there are several wonderful hotels including a trio of nautical-themed properties (the Victory, the Lord Nelson and the Lady Hamilton), the First Hotel Reisen and the Rica. For dinner, Le Rouge feels like a bit of *fin de siècle* Paris transported to Stockholm, while Frantzén/Lindeberg is where you come to experience the cutting edge of modern Nordic cuisine.

Dominating the island is the Royal Palace, the official residence of the Swedish Royal Family, which is made up of King Carl XVI Gustav, Queen Silvia, Crown Princess Victoria, Prince Carl Philip and Princess Madeleine. Don't expect to spot the royals, as they now live at Drottningholm Palace outside the city and only use this palace for official functions. But the changing of the guard still takes place each day and you can also tour the palace or visit the excellent museums located beneath it. Other attractions include the Tyska Kyrkan (German church) and the Nobel Museum.

Be sure to cross on to Riddarholmen, the small island that's attached to Gamla Stan on its western side. You'll recognize it by the church, which has a distinctive spire made of wrought iron. For many centuries this church was the burial place of Swedish monarchs, though now they not only live outside the city centre, but get buried outside it too. From Riddarholmen you can take in some of the best views of Stadshuset. The large white yacht permanently moored on its quayside is now a floating hotel and restaurant but it dates from the 1920s. It was given as an 18th birthday present to Barbara Hutton, the Woolworth heiress, who later married Cary Grant.

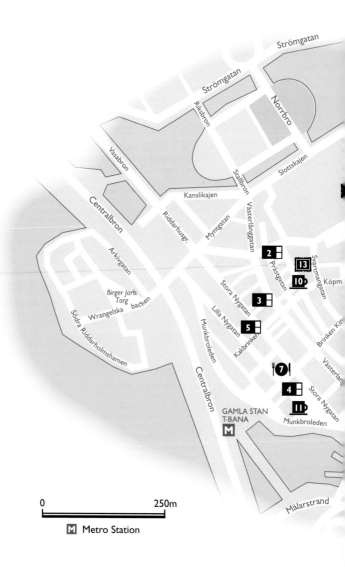

Östermalm

Östermalm is to Stockholm what the Upper East Side is to Manhattan or Mayfair to London. In other words, it's the posh bit where the old money lives.

The area is known for having some of the city's most expensive apartments. Living in Östermalm carries a certain cachet the other residents of Stockholm sometimes mock (and possibly envy). For younger Swedes there's even an Östermalm look, an unofficial uniform which over recent years has involved narrow Acne jeans, large J. Lindeberg belts, slim-fitting Filippa K shirts and elaborately arranged hairstyles that must take hours to get right. The girls are similarly style-conscious.

It's in Östermalm that you'll find some of the most exclusive shops, such as Svenskt Tenn, Sweden's most famous interior design store, and Modernity, the best place to buy Scandinavian furniture dating from the middle of the 20th century. Birger Jarlsgatan is crammed with international designer names – Versace, Gucci and their competitors. Here you'll also find the town's finest food market, Saluhall, as well as many fashionable bars and cafés. New venues regularly open (and close) alongside proven classics like Prinsen, Riche and Sturehof, which have been providing traditional Swedish food to the city's elite for more than a century.

Stureplan, a triangular plaza flanked by Birger Jarlsgatan and Sturegatan, is the axis around which all Stockholm nightlife seems to revolve. Many evenings begin beneath The Mushroom, a concrete structure in the middle of Stureplan that resembles a large fungus and is a popular meeting place. Standing on Stureplan you are just steps away from some of the town's coolest clubs, bars and restaurants. Östermalm is where you're most likely to run into models, pop stars, actors, footballers and junior members of the Royal Family enjoying a night out.

For visitors to the city, Östermalm has several excellent hotels, including the Diplomat and Esplanade, which stand side-by-side overlooking

the water on the city's most desirable stretch of real estate, Strandvägen. Then, of course, on the border of Norrmalm but with an Östermalm attitude, stands the Grand Hotel, which is where Nobel laureates check in when they come to get their medals and their 10 million kronor prize (around $1.5 million, €1 million or £795,000) from the King.

Östermalm is handy for visiting the National Museum, Nordic Museum and the Museum of Modern Art, which between them span several centuries of Swedish art, design and culture. Djurgården is a large island park adjoining Östermalm that is home to the city's two most-visited attractions: Skansen, an open air museum-zoo, and the not-to-be-missed Vasa Museum, which houses an incredibly well-preserved 17th-century warship that was salvaged from the waters of Stockholm harbour after it sank on its maiden voyage in 1628.

If you've come to enjoy great architecture, decadent nights out, excellent shopping and a big dollop of culture, you may find yourself reluctant to go anywhere else.

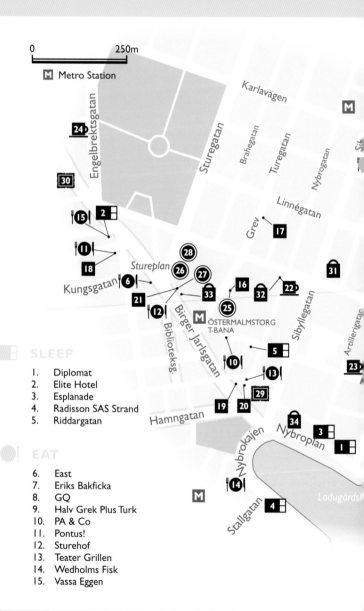

0 ⊢———┤ 250m

M Metro Station

Karlavägen

Engelbrektsgatan

Sturegatan

Brahegatan

Turegatan

Nybrogatan

Si

24

30

Linnégatan

Grev

17

15 **2**

11

18

Stureplan

28

31

26

Kungsgatan **6**

27

16

22

21

33

32

12

25

ÖSTERMALMSTORG
T-BANA

Birger Jarlsgatan

Biblioteksg.

Sibyllegatan

Artillerigatan

10

5

23

13

29

19 **20**

Hamngatan

34

3

Nybrokajen

Nybroplan

1

14

M

Stallgatan

4

Ladugårdsl

Östermalm local map

Karlavägen

Artillergatan

Karlaplan

Skeppargatan

Grevgatan

Linnégatan

Narvavägen

Humlegårdsgatan

Grevgatan

Styrmansgatan

Magnigatan

gatan

Riddargatan

Grev

Strandvägen

ken

9

7

Norrmalm/Vasastan

Norrmalm can be thought of as the city's business and shopping centre. Vasastan (or Vasastaden to use its full name) is a more residential area located to its north and west side. The boundary between the two of them is a blurry one, but taken together they include plenty of great stores, bars and restaurants.

Here you'll find the city's most exclusive department store, NK, as well as its more affordable competitor Åhléns. There's also the Opera House (right), which includes several places to eat and drink, and Hötorget, the outdoor market beside Konserthuset, which sells flowers and vegetables Monday to Saturday and then hosts a (not particularly good) flea market on Sundays. Drottninggatan is Stockholm's equivalent of Oxford Street: always bustling, usually depressing and best avoided.

When, in the late 1950s and early 1960s, Stockholm was seized with a madness for modernizing, Norrmalm was one of the areas that suffered the most. Things could have been worse, of course. One plan called for Gamla Stan to be been flattened in order to provide convenient parking for the rest of the city. Thankfully this was avoided but many old buildings were lost. Some made way for Kulturhuset (below), a vast cultural centre that is loved and loathed in equal measure.

You'll arrive in this part of town if you take the Arlanda Express from the airport to the city. Close to the Central Station is the Nordic Light hotel, one of the most quintessentially Scandinavian hotels in town.

From Norrmalm/Vasastan there are several bridges over to Kungsholmen, another of the main islands that make up the city. Until relatively recently, if tourists went to Kungsholmen at all it was just to visit Stadshuset (City Hall). Having toured the building and seen the room in which the Nobel banquet takes place, they would have crossed back to the Norrmalm/Vasastan. Now, though, Kungsholmen is worth exploring for its own sake. Although still largely residential, it has several attractive restaurants and a new found sense of confidence. If you can't decide what you'd like to eat, go to Scheelegatan, one of the best restaurant rows in the city. Here you can bounce from bar to bar until you decide which of the many restaurants you want to visit. Also on Scheelegatan is the First Hotel Amaranten, which is fairly priced and ideally located for easy access to the Central Station.

In the summer, Rålambshovsparken is the perfect place for a picnic (you could pick up some food at the nearby Muffin Bakery) and there are also plenty of places to go for a swim. Considering how close Kungsholmen is to the city centre, it would be a shame to visit the city and not to cross over to one of its most up-and-coming areas   .

SLEEP

1. Berns
2. Birger Jarl
3. Clarion Sign
4. Grand Hotel
5. Nordic Light
6. Nordic Sea
7. Stureplan

EAT

8. Bistro Berns
9. Den Gamle Och Havet
10. Divino
11. Esperanto
12. Fredsgatan 12
13. Mathias Dahlgren
14. Operahuset
15. Peacock Dinner Club
16. Prinsen
17. Vassa Eggen

DRINK

18. Absolut Ice Bar
19. Cadier Bar (Grand Hotel)
20. Inferno
21. Marden
22. Storstad

SNACK

23. Chokladfabriken
24. Gooh!
25. Martins Gröna
26. Non Solo Bar

PARTY

27. 235
28. Café Opera
29. Casino Cosmopol
30. F12 Terrassen
31. Fasching Jazz Club
32. Solidaritet
33. The White Room

CULTURE

34. Filmstaden
35. Grand Cinema
36. Hallwylska Museum
37. Kulturhuset
38. National Museum
39. Opera House

SHOP

39. Acne
    Biblioteksgatan
    Birger Jarlsgatan
40. Gallerian
    Hamngatan
41. Hötorget
42. NK
43. PUB
44. Åhléns

Norrtullsgatan

Karlsbergsvägen

Dalagatan

Vasmanna

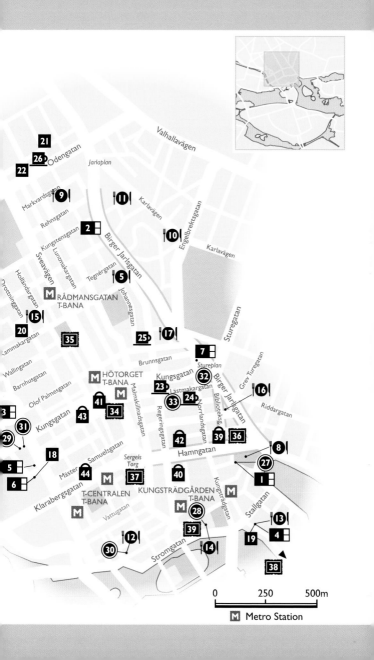

21
26 Odengatan
22
Jarlaplan
Valhallavägen
Markvardsgatan
9
11 Karlavägen
Rehnsgatan
2
10
Engelbrektsgatan
Kungstengatan
Lunmakargatan
Sveavägen
Birger Jarlsgatan
Karlavägen
Tegnérgatan
5
Drottninggatan
Hollandargatan
RÅDMANSGATAN
T-BANA
Johannesgatan
Sturegatan
15
20
35
25 17
Kammakargatan
Brunnsgatan
7
Wallingatan
Stureplan
Grev Turegatan
Barnhusgatan
HÖTORGET
T-BANA
Kungsgatan
32
Birger Jarlsgatan
16
Olof Palmesgatan
23
Läsmakargatan
24
Riddargatan
3
41
34
33
Biblioteksg
31
43
Regeringsgatan
Norrlandsgatan
39 36
29
Kungsgatan
42
8
18
Hamngatan
27
5
Mäster
Samuelsgatan
44
Sergels
Torg
40
1
6
37
T-CENTRALEN
T-BANA
KUNGSTRÄDGÅRDEN
T-BANA
13
Klarabergsgatan
28
4
Vattugatan
39
19
12
14
Stallgatan
30
Strömgatan
38
Kungsträdgården

0   250   500m

M Metro Station

Södermalm

Södermalm, or Söder as it is casually known, is the large island on Stockholm's southern side that feels like the most downtown part of the city. It is often thought of as the anti-Östermalm, the area with a younger, cooler demographic (a result of the lower rents), where bars are more likely to serve beer than cocktails, and where in place of exclusive restaurants and designer boutiques you're more likely to find yoga studios, second-hand shops and a sense of fashion that tends to be more street than chic.

Many tourists pop over to Söder just for the views. Close to the bridge crossing from the Old Town is Eriks Gondolen, the restaurant-bar suspended from a viewing platform, which is the perfect place for a sunset drink. Then, at the end of 2007, another restaurant-bar opened, Och Himlen Därtill, which takes things to a whole new level. It's located on the 25th and 26th floors of Skatteskrapan, which translates as The Tax Scraper, so named because it used to house the tax office. It is the tallest office building in the city, and the views from the top are astounding and vertigo inducing.

Söder's other attractions include one of the city's best hotels, the Rival, which is owned by Benny Andersson from Abba. The hotel brought fresh life to Mariatorget, the square on which it stands, thanks in part to the Rival Bakery and Rival Café which are next door to the lobby, while inside the hotel there's a classic Art Deco cinema and matching circular bar. On Söder's southern edge there's one of the city's biggest hotels, the Clarion, which is worth bearing in mind for leisure travel because their rates fall in the summer when business travel slumps.

Close to the Clarion there's Eriksdalsbadet, which has Stockholm's best indoor and outdoor swimming pools, and a beautiful waterside path runs along the western edge of Söder. In the summer this is one of the nicest places to go for a paddle outside.

For shopping, there are two key places to explore. Götgatan, the partially pedestrianized street leading towards Och Himlen Därtill, has several cool clothing shops on it. Then there's an area south of Folkungagatan that has been branded as SoFo. While it pales in comparison with New York's SoHo, which inspired its nickname, it's full of unusual independent stores.

By night Södermalm is extremely lively, with a great range of places to eat and a drink: Italian food from Portofino... cheap-but-excellent sushi from Akki... meatballs and beer at Pelikan... Or spend a night eating, drinking and dancing at Marie Laveau, an all-purpose venue that includes a restaurant, several bars and, at the weekend, a huge subterranean club.

From 2009 there will be another reason to visit Södermalm, with the opening of the city's most-anticipated new attraction – Abba: The Museum. More than a quarter century after Agnetha, Benny, Björn and Anni-Frid disbanded, they're still a force to be reckoned with.

Mamma mia! Here we go again.

Centralbron

Riddarfjärden

Mälarstrand

2

Bastugatan

Tavastgatan

Brännkyrkagatan

Torkel

Hornsgatan

5

9

Bellmansgatan

3

Skaraborgsgatan

ZINKENSDAMM
T-BANA

Knussonsg.

Sankt Paulsgatan

Björngårdsgatan

Kvarngatan

Krukmakargatan

ST PAULSGATAN
T-BANA

Yxkullsgatan

Timmermansgatan

Prästgårdsgatan

Högbergsgatan

Rosenlundsgatan

Maria

Svedenborgsgatan

Bangårdsg

Fatbursgatan

Södermalmsallén

Magnus Ladulåsgatan

SLEEP

1. Clarion
2. Hilton Slussen
3. Rival

EAT

4. Akki Sushi
5. Portofino

DRINK

6. Gondolen
7. Och Himlen Därtill
8. Pelikan

SNACK

9. Café Rival
10. Chokladfabriken

PARTY

11. Marie Laveau
12. Mosebacke
13. Patricia

SHOP

Götgatan

Hallandsgat

Södermalm local map

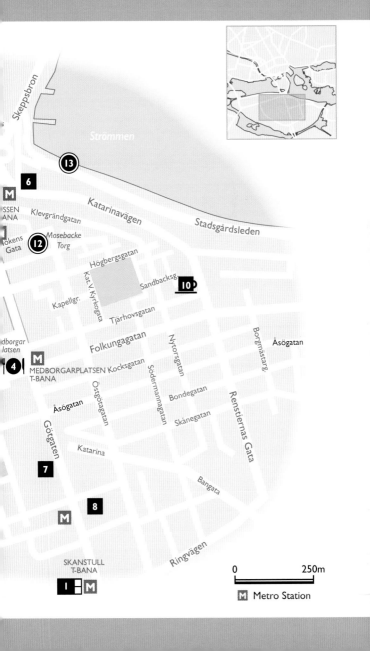

Skeppsbron

Strömmen

13

6

M

SSEN
ANA

Klevgrändgatan

Katarinavägen

Stadsgårdsleden

Tokens
Gata

12

Mosebacke
Torg

Högbergsgatan

Sandbacksg

10

Kat. V. Kyrkogata

Kapellgr.

Tjärhovsgatan

dborgar
latsen

4

M

MEDBORGARPLATSEN
T-BANA

Kocksgatan

Folkungagatan

Nytorgsgatan

Borgmästarg

Åsögatan

Östgötagatan

Södermannagatan

Bondegatan

Renstiernas Gata

Åsögatan

Skånegatan

Götgatan

Katarina

7

Bangata

8

M

SKANSTULL
T-BANA

Ringvägen

M

0   250m

M Metro Station

sleep...

It's fair to say that Stockholm is not one of the world's greatest hotel cities. It hasn't got the range and variety of places you might encounter in London, New York or Paris, for instance, nor the same sense of hotel romance. What's more, because it's so expensive to hire staff in Sweden you won't find lobbies swarming with eager bellhops or scores of people behind the concierge and check-in desks.

However, the hotels in Stockholm do benefit from the trio of Swedish passions: sleeping, eating and designing.

Maybe it's because of the long, cold winters, but Swedes pride themselves on their beds. The country is, after all, home to two luxury bed manufacturers: Hästens and Duxiana. As a consequence, you'll usually find an excellent mattress and good bed linen in your room, even in the more moderately priced hotels.

Following a good night's sleep, you can count on a good buffet breakfast to start the day. This will typically include Swedish cheeses, such as Västerbotten and Prästost, as well as lots of ham, various types of herring and healthy wholegrain breads.

Increasingly, the city's hotels are using the legendary Scandinavian sense of design to set themselves apart. This was pioneered by smaller hotels, such as the Berns, but the recently opened Clarion Sign (right), which is the biggest hotel to date in the city, is awash with furnishings by Arne Jacobsen, Hans Wegner and Norway Says.

For extravagant opulence in the city, your first choice would naturally be the Grand (right), which is where Nobel laureates lodge when they come to pick up their prizes. In 2007, it added another feather to its cap by opening the best restaurant in the city: Mathias Dahlgren (see Eat).

Other stand-out properties include the trendy Rival on Södermalm, which is owned by Benny from Abba; the minimalist Nordic Light close to the Central Station; the Hotel J, which feels like a little corner of New England in Scandinavia; and the best waterfront hotels, including the Esplanade, Diplomat and Radisson SAS Strand, on the condition that you get a room with a water view. Exciting new properties include the Stureplan, opening in 2008, and the Lydmar in 2009. The previous Lydmar, was one of the city's trendiest hotels; the new version is located next door to the Grand.

All the hotels in this section are of a high standard, whether they're conventional, contemporary or more unusual in style. Those that do not have plasma screens and DVD players make up for it in other ways.

Bear in mind that because Stockholm is a major conference venue, many hotels keep their rates high during the week when their clientele consists largely of business travellers. Rates at the weekend and in July, when Sweden takes its annual holiday, can be much lower, sometimes by almost 50%, particularly in hotels that primarily target non-leisure guests.

Prices given are the cost of a double room in low season to a suite in high season.

Our top 10 places to stay in Stockholm are:
1. Grand Hotel
2. Berns
3. Rival
4. Diplomat
5. Victory
6. Hotel J
7. Radisson SAS Strand
8. Nordic Light
9. Esplanade
10. Hilton Slussen

Our top 5 for style are:
1. Berns
2. Grand Hotel
3. Rival
4. Nordic Light
5. Hotel J

Our top 5 for atmosphere are:
1. Grand Hotel
2. Berns
3. Hotel J
4. Victory
5. Stallmästaregården

Our top 5 for location are:
1. Grand Hotel
2. Berns
3. Radisson SAS Strand
4. Esplanade
5. Diplomat

Berns, Berzelii Park, Norrmalm
Tel: 08 566 322 00 www.berns.se
Rates: 2,950–10,500kr

The Berns was originally established in 1863 as a centre for nightlife and entertainment (a role it retains to this day) but later added 65 modern, well-designed hotel rooms. They're simply furnished and incorporate lots of wood, which creates a modern, Scandinavian feel. Public spaces, in contrast, are spectacular. It's well worth dropping in for a cocktail at the bar, perhaps

en route to a viewing at the neighbouring Bukowskis auction house. The location of the Berns is perfect, in the very heart of the city. Just be aware that the hotel hosts a packed programme of club nights, not to mention shows and concerts at the Chinese theatre next door. This is a hotel to check in to if you want to feel connected to the pulse of the city, rather than safely removed from it. Check the hotel's website for coming events. Bistro Berns (see Eat) is a charming choice for lunch or dinner.

Style 9, Atmosphere 9, Location 9

Birger Jarl, Tulegatan 8, Norrmalm
Tel: 08 674 1800 www.birgerjarl.se
Rates: 1,090–5,500kr

At first sight the Birger Jarl (which takes its name from the 13th-century statesman credited with establishing Stockholm as the country's capital) can seems rather bland. The hotel is housed in a spectacularly uninteresting 1970s building, but when you step inside you'll notice that there's an emphasis on modern Swedish design. Among the standard rooms, which are furnished with simple furniture and white walls, there is a series of individually styled rooms all created by different Swedish designers. Room 709, for instance, is also called Miss Dottie and has walls covered with polka dots. Some rooms work well, but others seem to be more about the ego of the designer than the comfort of the guest, so it's wise to check the website to confirm what your room looks like. Although it's on a rather drab street, the Birger Jarl is handily located for access to the nightlife of both Östermalm and Vasastan.

Style 7, Atmosphere 6, Location 6

Clarion Hotel Stockholm, Ringvägen 98, Södermalm
Tel: 08 462 1000 www.clarionstockholm.com
Rates: 1,295–10,000kr

Although primarily a business hotel, the Clarion has much to recommend it.

The spacious, light-filled public areas and bedrooms are well proportioned and trendily furnished. The bar is busy with an after-work crowd most nights of the week and the fitness centre is luxurious enough for an hour or so of training. The hotel overlooks a busy motorway, but thanks to the sound-proofing this view, seen from the upstairs bar, takes on a certain grandeur. The drawback is the location, on the southern edge of Södermalm. It's perfect for exploring Söder (or swimming at the city's finest pool, which is just steps away), but less convenient for trips around the city centre or to the airport. Still, because it caters mainly to business travellers the hotel's rates at the weekend and on holidays are a steal.

Style 7, Atmosphere 6, Location 5

Clarion Sign, Östra Järnvägsgatan, Vasastan
Tel: 08 676 9800   www.clarionsign.com
Rates: 1,525kr–7,600kr

When it opened in February 2008, the 558-room Clarion Sign became Stockholm's biggest hotel. Although primarily targeting business travellers who appreciate its proximity to the Central Station and the Arlanda

Express, the hotel is worth knowing about even if you're not in town for a conference or a kick-off. For one thing, the hotel is far from bland. It's a monolithic building of black stone and glass. The design of the exterior echoes the pattern of the railway tracks that run alongside it. Inside there's a spa on the 8th floor and, off the lobby, the Aquavit Grill & Raw Bar. This is a spin-off from Aquavit in New York City, a Swedish restaurant run by Marcus Samuelsson, an Ethiopian-born, Swedish-raised chef. Of course, no one would come to the Clarion for a romantic weekend, but its location and sleek design make up for the lack of real charm.

Style 7, Atmosphere 7, Location 7

Diplomat, Strandvägen 7c, Östermalm
Tel: 08 459 6800   www.diplomathotel.com
Rates: 2,095–4,995kr

The Diplomat enjoys a prime location on Strandvägen, one of the most desirable addresses in the city, and is an easy walk from Östermalm and convenient for Djurgården. The building retains many of its original features, including beautiful stained-glass windows in the stairwell, but it has success-

fully combined them with modern bedrooms and lively public spaces. The lounge-bar, T/Bar, is popular with the affluent office workers of Östermalm each evening, in part because there's often a happy hour on bottles of champagne during the week. Locals also like to come here for afternoon tea and, at the weekend, brunch. Don't miss the less-well-known cocktail bar, which is hidden away up a flight of stairs from the lobby. It's wonderfully old-fashioned and usually far less raucous than T/Bar. Needless to say, if you're checking in for a few days be sure to request a room with a view over the water.

Style 8, Atmosphere 8, Location 9

Elite Hotel, Birger Jarlsgatan 29, Östermalm
Tel: 08 566 22000 www.elite.se
Rates: 1,050–5,200kr

You'll find at least one Elite hotel in most of the major Swedish cities, from Luleå in the north to Malmö in the south. There are two in Stockholm, but

this is the only one to consider (don't confuse it with the Elite Palace, which is located on a dull street at the far end of Vasastan). As one of the hotels closest to Stureplan, the Elite Plaza is a good choice if you want proximity to the city's nightlife or the main shopping streets. It's housed in a beautiful, ornate building dating from 1884 that would look quite at home in any Parisian *arrondissement*, though the interior is less ostentatious than the exterior would suggest. The best rooms to get are those right on the corner of the building with a mini-balcony. In the same building you'll find one of Stockholm's best restaurants, Vassa Eggen (see Eat).

Style 7, Atmosphere 6, Location 8

Esplanade, Strandvägen 7A, Östermalm
Tel: 08 663 0740 www.hotelesplanade.se
Rates: 1,395–2,295kr

The Esplanade stands next door to the Diplomat and while from the outside they appear to be quite similar their interiors are markedly different. The Esplanade is, in the very best sense, old-fashioned. That is to say it's unconcerned with seeming like a hip, happening hotel. You won't find

enormous flatscreen TVs, a hopping bar scene or a state-of-the-art business centre here. Instead it prefers to base its reputation on personal service and genuine charm. The building has retained lots of original features dating from when the hotel opened in 1910. The décor is traditional and distinctly Swedish. You can spot the influence (and fabrics) of Svenskt Tenn, the country's most prestigious interior décor store, which is located on the same street. Considering its location, prices are extremely good. This is the sort of place you come to for quiet days, not wild nights.

Style 7, Atmosphere 7, Location 9

First Hotel Amaranten, Kungsholmsgatan 31, Kungsholmen
Tel: 08 692 5200   www.firsthotels.se
Rates: 2,090–70,000kr

The First Hotel's logo, a winged elephant, seems an appropriate symbol for this formerly frumpy hotel, which has taken flight as a fashionable but affordable place to stay on Kungsholmen. A thorough renovation a few years ago gave the hotel a boutique atmosphere, or as much of a boutique atmosphere as a hotel can have when it is a member of Scandinavia's biggest hotel chain and has 423 rooms. There's a (small) spa and the lobby bar is packed at the weekend, thanks in part to the hotel's proximity of Scheelegatan, one of the most restaurant-packed streets in the city. Within minutes of walking out of the lobby you can take your pick of a variety of cuisines, including Indian, American, French and Swedish, as well as a slew of bars that are busy

from the minute the working day ends.

Style 6, Atmosphere 6, Location 6

First Hotel Reisen, Skeppsbron 12, Gamla Stan

Tel: 08 223 260 www.firsthotels.se
Rates: 1,550–6,000kr

While the other Gamla Stan hotels noted in this chapter are in the heart of the Old Town, this 144-room property stands on the waterfront where you can watch the ferries setting sail for Finland, Estonia and beyond. The building dates from the 17th century but the public spaces were recently renovated to give them plenty of 21st-century attitude. The restaurant has black-and-white striped walls and lots of dramatic black furniture. Like its sister property, the Amaranten on Kungsholmen, the bar attracts plenty of non-

residents. During the summer the outdoor seating is popular. Bedrooms are a little bit frumpy but the exposed brick in some adds charm in keeping with the age of the building. What's more the views are enviable and the location is convenient, as the hotel is just steps from the Royal Palace.

Style 6, Atmosphere 7, Location 8

Grand Hotel, S Blasieholmshammen 8, Östermalm
Tel: 08 679 3500   www.grandhotel.se
Rates: 2,090–70,000kr

Originally opened in 1874, the Grand's neo-classical façade topped with fluttering flags is one of the city's landmarks. Over recent years it has spruced

itself up and reinforced its standing as the city's most prestigious property. The location and the calibre of the service are terrific, while the restaurant (Mathias Dahlgren, see Eat) and bar (Cadier Bar, see Drink) are both superb and should be visited by anyone coming to Stockholm. The waterfront setting opposite the Palace affords beautiful views. Needless to say, it's only really worth staying here if you can afford a room with a water view; you're better off in a good room at another hotel than a bad room-without-a-view here. If money is no object, try the Princess Lilian Suite, named after a Welsh-born member of the Swedish Royal Family, with its own private cinema. This is where the Nobel laureates lodge before picking up their prizes from the King.

Style 9, Atmosphere 9, Location 9

Hilton Slussen, Guldgränd, Södermalm
Tel: 08 517 35300 www.hilton.com
Rates: 1,190–5,890kr

Let's be honest: from the outside, the Hilton is quite appallingly ugly. What was the Stockholm planning board thinking? Having said that, when you are inside the building looking out, it is a far more pleasant experience. For one

thing, the hotel has glorious views over Riddarfjärden towards Gamla Stan. All the bedrooms are smartly furnished and the suites are a treat: spacious, airy, with modern furniture and marble bathrooms. The distinctive use of light and dark striped wood in the corridors and bedrooms gives the hotel a distinct personality and there's a great gym and a decent restaurant. Needless to say, it's a popular hotel for business travellers from North America but locals do drop in to visit the bar, attracted by amazing views. The location is handy if you want to explore Södermalm or Gamla Stan.

Style 8, Atmosphere 8, Location 7

Hotel J, Ellensviksvägen 1, Nacka Strand
Tel: 08 601 3000 www.hotelj.se
Rates: 1,190–3,495kr

The Hotel J combines waterfront tranquillity with bags of style and first-class service. The atmosphere makes it feel like a wonderfully comfortable private home, with a blue-and-white colour scheme that's reminiscent of a New England sailing club. (The hotel is named after the J-class range of yachts.) In the winter it's comforting, with blazing fires and plates of

croissants and cakes available most of the day, but it's at its best in the summer when you can dine outside watching fleets of yachts sailing into and out of the city. It's located a short ferry ride from the city, so perhaps it's not ideal for someone on a first visit to Stockholm who wants to dash around town, but perfect for anyone wanting a more relaxed pace of life. The hotel's sister property at Gåshaga is further removed from town but equally pleasant.

Style 9, Atmosphere 9, Location 7

Hotel Riddargatan, Riddargatan 14, Östermalm
Tel: 08 555 73000 www.hotelriddargatan.se
Rates: 1,425–4,600kr

The main advantage of this 45-room hotel, which is part of a group of Swedish and Danish properties, is its location. Yes, it has understated but

tasteful décor and, yes, the staff are friendly, but its main draw is its setting right in the heart of Östermalm. Even the lack of a restaurant is almost a blessing. After all, why would you eat dinner here when you are just seconds away from dropping in to Riche (see Drink), PA and Co (see Eat), and Grodan (see Drink/Party). It's also an easy walk straight along the street to Riddarbageriet (see Snack) where you can buy the best bread in the city or grab a light lunch. The hotel does, however, have a cheerful red-lit bar in the centre of what serves as the breakfast room from 7am to 11am.

Style 7, Atmosphere 6, Location 8

Lady Hamilton Hotel, Storkyrkobrinken 5, Gamla Stan
Tel: 08 506 40100   www.ladyhamiltonhotel.se
Rates: 1,850–2,850kr

Lord Nelson Hotel, Västerlånggatan 22, Gamla Stan
Tel: 08 506 40120   www.lordnelsonhotel.se
Rates: 1,490–2,150kr

Named after the British naval hero and his mistress, the Lord Nelson and Lady Hamilton are two of three Old Town hotels owned by the Bengtsson family (the other being the Victory). Both hotels ooze traditional charm and are full to overflowing with model ships, compasses, naval antiques, painted chests, grandfather clocks, crystal lighting, oriental carpets and bedrooms crammed with all sorts of trinkets and knick-knacks. As you can imagine, neither hotel is the place for fans of Swedish minimalism. However, the cheerfully cluttered interiors seem to be in keeping with thespirit of Gamla Stan, though be aware that they are on streets that can be clogged

with pedestrians. The Lord Nelson has 29 rooms which have portholes in the doors and are named after famous ships; it's normally the more affordable hotel. The Lady Hamilton has 34 rooms named after wildflowers and a 14th-century well in the basement.

Style 7, Atmosphere 8, Location 7

Nordic Light, Vasaplan, Norrmalm
Tel: 08 505 63000   www.nordichotels.se
Rates: 1,730–4,300kr

The Nordic Light stands next to the Central Station, just steps from the Arlanda Express rail link that can take you from the city to the airport in just 20 minutes. Because of its proximity to the train, it's a haven for business travellers during the week but at the weekend leisure travellers move

in. The Nordic Light is one of the most stylish hotels in the city and, as its name suggests, light is the key element of the décor. Theatrical lighting is used to project colourful patterns onto the stark white walls. The bedrooms are compact but with wonderful beds, and the same light-on-white-walls theme makes them feel a bit more spacious. While the hotel's immediate surroundings are fairly drab, the entrance to the subway is right outside the hotel so it's easy to reach Stockholm's more interesting quarters. The hotel stands opposite its non-identical twin, the Nordic Sea.

Style 9, Atmosphere 7, Location 7

Nordic Sea, Vasaplan, Norrmalm

Tel: 08 505 63000 www.nordichotels.se
Rates: 1,120–3,800kr

The Nordic Sea is not as style-conscious as the Nordic Light, nor is it as expensive. However, if you are trying to save kronor bear in mind that the

cheapest of its rooms are the size of a shoe box and do not even have exterior windows. The hotel's marine theme is reflected in the predominantly blue-and-white colour palette and the large and impressive aquarium that dominates the lobby. However, the Sea's biggest attraction is the Ice Bar, where you have to wear fur-lined parkas to cope with the constant −10°C. The walls are made of ice, the tables are made of ice, the stools are made of ice and, yes, you drink chilled vodka out of ice glasses. The concept is not the novelty it once was, but it's still extremely popular and you need to buy tickets in advance to get in.

Style 7, Atmosphere 6, Location 7

Radisson SAS Strand, Nybrokajen 9, Östermalm

Tel: 08 5066 4000 www.radisson.com
Rates: 1,945–10,000kr

The 152-room Strand, which was completed in time for the 1912 Stockholm Olympics, is one of the best hotels in the Radisson SAS chain. It has breathtaking views and a super-convenient location in the centre of the city, an easy walk from Östermalm, Gamla Stan and the shops on Hamngatan. Inside, you'll find a relaxed, pleasant lobby and a restaurant

that's great for dinner or weekend brunch. As with all of Stockholm's waterfront hotels, it's worth splurging on a room with a view, but at the Strand you should go a step further and book into one of the Water View suites. To open up their double-height windows on a summer's day and gaze out over the quayside is a memorable experience. Alternatively, if it's a very special visit – and if funds allow – why not take the spectacular two-floor Tower Suite which has its own private terrace.

Style 8, Atmosphere 7, Location 9

Rica Hotel Gamla Stan, Lilla Nygatan 25, Gamla Stan
Tel: 08 723 7250 www.rica.se
Rates: 995–2,795kr

The Rica chain has dozens of hotels throughout Norway and Sweden. Of

the company's four properties in and around Stockholm, this one in Gamla Stan is by far the best for people who are travelling for pleasure rather than business. As befits a hotel in the Old Town, the rooms and suites are elegantly furnished in a traditional fashion, reminiscent of the 18th century (though the building is even older, dating from the 1650s). Rooms have rich fabrics and classical prints on the walls, and some even have brass beds. The hotel's main asset is its location: you step straight out onto one of the cobbled streets of the Old Town but, thankfully, not one that is permanently swamped with tourists. Once you check in it's easy to forget that you are in one of the biggest cities in Scandinavia.

Style 7, Atmosphere 7, Location 8

Rival, Mariatorget 3, Södermalm

Tel: 08 5457 8900 www.rival.se
Rates: 1,590–8,950kr

Owned by Benny Andersson from Abba, a man who knows a thing or two about making a hit, the Rival is quite unlike anything else in the city. It has 99

rooms, a cinema with classic red velvet seating and an art deco cocktail bar. Its personality carries over to two adjoining businesses, the Rival Café and the Rival Bakery, which is one of the best bakeries in the city. The hotel's décor is inspired by Swedish films and every room features a still taken from a Swedish movie (including, of course, *Abba: The Movie*). Bedrooms have pillow menus, as well as flatscreen TVs and DVD players. When it opened, the Rival revitalized the Mariatorget square on which it stands and it remains one of the city's hippest hotels. It's particularly good for visitors who want to spend their time exploring the slightly more alternative scene on Södermalm.

Style 9, Atmosphere 8, Location 8

Stallmästaregården, Norrtull, Stockholm
Tel: 08 610 1300 www.stallmastaregarden.se
Rates: 1,195–4,900kr

The Stallmästaregården is an unusual place. It's just an easy taxi ride from the city centre but it stands on the edge of Haga Park and feels like it's out in the middle of the Swedish countryside. It's so romantic and rustic that it's

 a popular venue for weddings throughout the summer. At first glance, the hotel's décor seems very like that of a country house hotel, complete with chandeliers and period portraits decorating the reception area. But when you get to the rooms you'll find they are far more modern, with lots of strong colours and bold fabrics. Some of the funkier rooms are split level with a sleeping area upstairs and a living room below. The restaurant is known for its traditional Swedish dishes and in the warmer months you can dine outdoors and take in the marvellous park views. An excellent choice if you want to feel as if you're in the country but still have access to the attractions of the city.

Style 8, Atmosphere 9, Location 6

Stureplan, Birger Jarlsgatan 24, Östermalm
Tel: 08 768 0877 www.hotelstureplan.se
Rates: 2,350–3,450kr

This new 102-room hotel close to Stureplan is slated to open in 2008. It's housed in a 19th-century building with décor that fuses the 18th and 21st centuries: classic rooms are furnished in the traditional Swedish Gustavian

style while loft rooms are minimalist with polished concrete floors. There are also tiny, low-price windowless cabins intended for businessmen who just want to arrive late, leave early, and don't care about a city view. The location is ideal for nightlife, with Stureplan a moment's walk away, shopping on Birger Jarlsgatan or eating. Both Pontus! and Vassa Eggen (see Eat) are almost within spitting distance. After a tiring night out residents can get reduced-price entry to Sturebadet, the city's most exclusive spa. Should you

prefer not to go out, you can always just hang out in the hotel's champagne bar.

Style n/a, Atmosphere n/a, Location 8

Victory Hotel, Lilla Nygatan 5, Gamla Stan
Tel: 08 5064 0000 www.victoryhotel.se
Rates: 2,150–7,500kr

The Victory Hotel is named after Horatio Nelson's flagship and has a degree more opulence than its two sibling properties, the Lord Nelson and the Lady Hamilton. The nautical knick-knacks remain at the Victory (including a

letter written by Nelson in which he complains of seasickness), but here the rooms are named after Swedish sea captains and the suites are wildly opulent with huge four-poster beds and graceful sitting rooms in which Bang & Olufsen TVs and stereos sit alongside 17th-century elegance. There's a mural on the ceiling of the Captain Johansson suite, which hasn't been altered since 1640. If you find yourself unable to move far from such luxury, no problem: the Leijontornet restaurant downstairs is one of the finest in the city. The excellent wine cellar sits among the remains of Stockholm's fortification walls. This hotel offers sheer indulgence in the middle of Gamla Stan.

Style 8, Atmosphere 9, Location 8

Villa Källhagen, Djurgårdsbrunnsvägen 10, Östermalm
Tel: 08 665 0300 www.kallhagen.se
Rates: 1,590–3,000kr

Villa Källhagen is tucked away in an area of rolling parkland just east from the heart of Östermalm and across the water from Djurgården. There's been an inn here since 1810, though the current building dates from 1990. It's a small place, with only 36 rooms, so you should be sure to book well in advance during busy periods. Each room has panoramic views of the park and is charmingly furnished – you'll spot the distinctive Josef Frank fabrics from Svenskt Tenn (see Shop). If you're happier in peaceful green

surroundings than the hubbub of the city, it's a good choice. You won't be disturbed by street noise, yet it's just a short taxi ride to the middle of town. The two restaurants are known for the quality of their food and serve a popular weekend brunch.

Style, 7, Atmosphere 7, Location 6

eat...

The restaurants of Stockholm are rather like the residents of Stockholm: friendly but not overly exuberant; attractive but rarely extravagant; generally intelligent but seldom showy; Scandinavian to the core but strongly influenced by other countries and open to new trends.

Swedes tend to travel a lot, and this is reflected in the range of cooking on offer. The majority of places stick to what could be termed modern international cuisine but they also offer the Swedish staples. It's not unusual to find spaghetti carbonara and Thai curry on the same menu as meatballs with lingonberries or an elk stew. While prices are undeniably high, so are standards. Stockholmers are proud of the city's restaurants, and rightly so.

During the week you might find that some of the restaurants seem to be rather quiet. This is because the locals tend to eat at home with family and friends. The desire to go out comes into force at weekends. This is not to say that from Monday to Thursday you'll find places empty or populated entirely by tourists, but just that the weekend is when you'll feel the most authentic Stockholm vibe.

Bear in mind that Stockholm is a seasonal city – in the warm summer months the emphasis is on sitting outside, eating lightly and sipping a glass of wine. When winter returns, and the temperature plummets, everybody crowds indoors to feast on more robust meat dishes, washed down with heavy red wine or beer.

If you want to experience the very best of Scandinavian dining, you'll find outstanding food presented by super-proficient staff in rooms that display some of that famous Scandinavian design flair. Lunch on the terrace at Lux, an evening at Esperanto or Edsbacka Krog, dinner with a view of the Royal Palace at Mathias Dahlgren (currently the most thrilling restaurant in the city) are well worth the bruising they will give your credit card.

For dinner, most kitchens are open between 5pm and 11pm. For lunch, service usually begins at around 11.30am and goes on until 2.30pm. Ever punctual, the majority of Swedes take an hour's lunch that starts promptly at noon, so it's wise to avoid the midday crush by dining a little later.

Tipping is not necessary at lunchtime. In the evening it is appreciated – though not compulsory. Because weekends tend to be busy, and summer weekends in particular can be insane, a reservation is always advisable, no matter where you are going. And if a place is new or particularly popular, you should book well in advance.

Top 10 restaurants in Stockholm:

1. Mathias Dahlgren
2. Edsbacka Krog
3. Esperanto
4. Lux
5. Den Gyldene Freden
6. Operahuset
7. Vassa Eggen
8. Wedholms Fisk
9. Fredsgatan 12
10. Prinsen

Top 5 restaurants for food:

1. Mathias Dahlgren
2. Edsbacka Krog
3. Esperanto
4. Lux
5. Wedholms Fisk

Top 5 restaurants for service:

1. Mathias Dahlgren
2. Edsbacka Krog
3. Esperanto
4. Fredsgatan 12
5. Lux

Top 5 restaurants for atmosphere:

1. Mathias Dahlgren
2. Den Gyldene Freden
3. Operahuset
4. Le Rouge
5. Sturehof

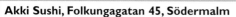

Akki Sushi, Folkungagatan 45, Södermalm

Tel: 08 643 3377

Open: daily, 11am (1pm Sat, 4pm Sun)   125kr

Sushi

Yes, it's tiny, with only five seats. And no, it's not glamorous. It's found right
by the entrance to the Medborgarplatsen subway, with no sign in the window, and they often play the music too loudly. It is, to be honest, a scruffy
little hole-in-the-wall. And as is so often the way with scruffy little hole-in-
the-walls, it's wonderful. Generally speaking, Stockholm is a sushi wilderness,

which is unforgivable when you bear in mind that this city is awash with the
freshest possible seafood, but Akki stands apart from the crowd. Don't plan
a night around it because word of its excellence has spread and so you can
never bank on getting one of those few seats. Either phone ahead to
arrange some sushi to collect, or else if you're passing by (perhaps en route
to Och Himlen Därtill, see Drink) and you see a free space then grab it.

Food 8, Service 6, Atmosphere 5

Bistro Berns, Berzelii Park, Norrmalm

Tel: 08 5663 2515 www.bistroberns.se   575kr

Open: 11.30am–midnight Mon–Fri; noon–midnight Sat; noon–8pm Sun

French

This modern little glass building in Berzelii Park, the patch of green just in
front of the Berns Hotel, has changed identity several times over the years.
But now, as Bistro Berns, a cosy French bistro with a simple menu and

friendly staff, it seems to have hit its stride. It has appropriated all the trappings of a traditional bistro – zinc and mahogany surfaces, crisp white table cloths, lighting that flatters the patrons, waiters clad in black and white, bottles of wine chilling in large silver bowls. The menu, which changes daily, features all the classics, like cassoulet, *croque monsieur*, *moules frites*, snails, oysters and *entrecôte de Café Paris*, all at prices that are fair. Stockholm has had something of a bistro boom of late, and Bistro Berns is one of the best. Its location in the heart of the city means that it's always popular so be sure to book a table.

Food 8, Service 7, Atmosphere 7

Den Gamle och Havet, Tulegatan 27, Vasastan
Tel: 08 661 5300   www.visomkanmat.se
Open: daily 5.30pm–midnight (10.30pm Sun)   455kr
Italian

'The Old Man and the Sea' takes its name from the huge painting that dominates the dining room. A couple of years ago it moved from its previous home in Östermalm to larger premises located about a five minute walk from Odenplan. A tiny little bit of the charm of the old restaurant was lost in the process, but it gained more space and the excellence of the food and friendliness of the staff remain undimmed. Go when you are really hungry and want authentic Italian. Be warned that portions are ample. Rabbit *alla cacciatore*, liver with cream and cognac, *tortiglioni* with four types of cheese, a perfect caramel *panna cotta*… no one gets thin dining here. The steaming bowl of fish soup, shared between the table, is particularly wonderful.

Food 7, Service 8, Atmosphere 6

Den Gyldene Freden, Österlånggatan 51, Gamla Stan
Tel: 08 249 760 www.gyldenefreden.se
Open: 11.30am–2.30pm, 5–11pm Mon–Fri; 1–11pm Sat   750kr
French/Swedish

'The Golden Peace' is one of the city's best-known restaurants and also one of the oldest restaurants in the world. It's been in business since 1722, taking its name from a peace accord signed with Russia in 1721. The interior is wonderfully atmospheric, with wooden beams, candlelit tables, and the ghosts of Swedish poets all around you. (Carl Michael Bellman, a famous 18th-century poet and composer, often dined here.) These days regular

diners include the members of the Swedish Academy, the people who pick the Nobel Prize winners, who regularly meet for lunch here. If you want the full experience, then come and enjoy some of the rich Franco–Swedish cuisine – pork belly with langoustines, sea buckthorn and liquorice *jus*, or a garlicky lamb stew. However, you can also just pop in for a glass of champagne at the small bar at the back of the dining room.

Food 8, Service 8, Atmosphere 9

Divino, Karlavägen 28, Östermalm
Tel: 08 611 0269 www.divino.se
Open: 6pm–11pm Mon–Sat. Closed Sundays and July.   830kr
Italian

Don't expect red-chequered tablecloths and candles in bottles at this neighbourhood Italian. Not when the neighbourhood in question is Östermalm, which is home to the upper echelons of Stockholm society. When Divino opened it was the first fine-dining Italian in town, and claims to be the city's

largest purchaser of truffles. The combination of decadent Tuscan food, liberal use of luxury ingredients, a huge wine list featuring dozens of champagnes, and an elegant dining room decorated with cream-and-gold walls and crystal lighting has proved to be a winning combination. Prices are steep, certainly, but you'll feel you had value for money and the service is great. However, if you'd prefer to experience the chef's expertise at lower prices and don't mind sitting in less opulent surroundings, opt for the

Divino Deli next door. It's particularly good for lunch on a summer's day when you can sit outside.

Food 8, Service 7, Atmosphere 6

East, Stureplan 13, Östermalm
Tel: 08 611 4959 www.east.se
Open: daily, 11.30am (5pm Sat/Sun)–1am   580kr
Asian

This always-busy restaurant serves sushi, sashimi and other Japanese,

Vietnamese and Korean dishes. It caters in large part to the people who go out to the bars and clubs around Stureplan, the square that marks the heart of Stockholm nightlife. Its location means that it's a popular place for people to meet up at the start of the evening, grab some food midway through a night out, or pop into for one last drink from the sake menu. The restaurant may close at 1am but the bar stays open until 3am every night of the week and there's usually a DJ playing. The sound, the lighting, the décor and the crowd are all very cool, but despite this the food is reasonably priced and good quality.

Food 7, Service 6, Atmosphere 7

Edsbacka Krog, Sollentunavägen 220, Sollentuna
Tel: 08 963 300 www.edsbackakrog.se
Open: 5.30pm–midnight Mon–Fri; 2pm–midnight Sat   1,100kr
Swedish

Edsbacka Krog is one of the finest restaurants in the land, so it's well worth taking a 15-minute taxi ride to get here. There has been a business on the site since 1626, starting with a coaching inn, but the current owner, Christer Lingström (a chef so famous in his homeland that he has appeared on a

 postage stamp), opened this restaurant in 1983. He earned his first Michelin star in 1992, with a second one to follow in 2000. The building retains the appearance of a traditional

Swedish inn, and the seasonal menu draws on local ingredients. You might find cured trout with lemon and fish roe, halibut wrapped in a potato crepe, or a pastry of green apples perfumed with cinnamon and nuts. You come here for an entire evening, and will need to book a table well in advance. A more affordable experience is available at Edsbacka Bistro, which is located opposite the main restaurant.

Food 10, Service 9, Atmosphere 8

Eriks Bakficka, Fredrikshovsgatan 4, Östermalm

Tel: 08 660 1599 www.eriks.se
Open: 11.30am–3pm Mon–Fri; 5–11pm (midnight Thurs–Sat).   565kr
Swedish Fusion

Erik Lallerstedt's other restaurant, Gondolen, is far better known, thanks to offering one of the best views in the city. But lovely as Gondolen is, particularly for a drink (see Drink), 'Erik's Backpocket' is a pleasanter choice for dinner. It's tucked away on a quiet street in Östermalm, close to the bridge crossing over to Djurgården, which makes it a good choice for lunch after a morning at the Vasa Museum. The décor is traditional, with a black-and-white tiled floor and wood panelled walls. The menu largely follows suit,

with lots of beef, pork and veal, but with occasional foreign influences creeping in, such as lemongrass-marinated chicken skewers with peanut sauce and basmati rice. The lunch menu changes weekly and at just over 100kr it's good value considering the quality of the food and how pleasant the atmosphere is. Ask for a table in the bar room.

Food 7, Service 7, Atmosphere 7

Esperanto, Kungstensgatan 2, Vasastan

Tel: 08 696 2323   www.esperantorestaurant.se
Open: 6pm–midnight Tues–Sat
International   1,440kr

Located on the second floor of a building adjoining the ballet academy, you could walk past Esperanto and not know it was there. But from the minute

you step inside, you realize you're in for a treat. The room is calm and elegant, the service flawless, and the food dazzling. Diners are given a choice of
two set menus, which are changed regularly, with dishes like *langoustine au
coraille* in an ocean mist with frozen vinaigrette; frozen white onion with
apple, celeriac and dried beef; or white winter vegetables with seared foie
gras and jasmine-perfumed dashi. The chefs, Sayan Isaksson and Daniel
Höglander, had the idea for the restaurant while on a fishing boat off the
coast of Cuba. They picked the name after they found a mention of the
international language in Paulo Coehlo's book *The Alchemist*. Their plan is to
blend elements from many nations' cuisines to create a totally new dining
experience. Yes, it's expensive, but it's exceptionally good in any language.

Food 9, Service 9, Atmosphere 7

Fjäderholmarnas Krog, Stora Fjäderholmen
Tel: 08 718 3355   www.fjaderholmarnaskrog.se
Open: Closed winter, except for Christmas.   765kr
Swedish/Seafood

If time allows, any visitor to Stockholm should venture out into the archipelago for lunch at some rustic inn on one of the islands. The trouble is, you
really need to allow a whole day to do so. If time is short, or you'd rather

spend your visit exploring the city, you can get a taste of the archipelago
experience by sailing for just 30 minutes from the centre of the city to
Fjäderholmarna (the Feather Islands). Here you can eat on the deck at a
classic red wooden building, right beside the waves, and watch the ferries

heading out to the islands. It's best to have a reservation but if you don't, try to be first off the ferry and walk briskly to the restaurant and you'll often be able to snag a table. Needless to say, seafood is the thing to order here.

Food 7, Service 6, Atmosphere 8

Frantzén/Lindeberg, Lilla Nygatan 21, Gamla Stan
Tel: 08 208 580 www.frantzen-lindeberg.com
Open: 6pm–1am Tues–Sat   1,640kr
Gourmet

A few years ago a tiny restaurant called Mistral opened on a sleepy street in the Old Town. It was an immediate success, earning both a Michelin star and a three-month waiting list. Then Mistral's owners decided they wanted a change. Björn Frantzén and Daniel Lindeberg took over and launched their

own restaurant that continues the tradition of excellence. They both know a thing or two about quality, having worked at L'Arpégè, Le Manoir aux Quat'Saisons, Edsbacka Krog (see page 57) and Riddarbageriet (see Snack). The two menus (choose 10 or 20 courses) are both filled with surprises: shoulder of pork with winter truffle, pollen and snail caviar; Jerusalem artichoke in two textures with hazlenut flour and a hint of licorice; and 'elastic' Amapucha chocolate with bitter chocolate oil, roasted sesame ice-cream and grilled marshmallows. Bear in mind the 20-course menu can take around four hours to eat, so plan your evening accordingly.

Food 9, Service 8, Atmosphere 7

Fredsgatan 12, Fredsgatan 12, Norrmalm

Tel: 08 248 052   www.fredsgatan12.com
Open: 11.30am–2pm Mon–Fri; 5pm–1am Mon–Sat   850kr
Swedish

F12 stands out for both its food and its appearance. It's one of the most
fashionable restaurants in the city, yet also one of the few to have been
awarded a Michelin star; Fredsgatan 12 (it takes its name from its address) is

a sibling to Kungsholmen (see page 64) and Le Rouge (see page 71). The
dining room's tasting menu classes dishes as either traditional or innovative.
For instance, on the traditional side you might find reindeer with juniper
berries and pearl onions while the innovative menu offers sirloin steak with
plums and dehydrated wine vinegar. This is the sort of place where you'll
see sharply dressed executives abusing their company credit cards to take
clients to lunch. There's also an equally stylish lounge-bar with a separate
menu. All summer long, the steps outside the restaurant function as hopping
outdoor bar, F12 Terrassen (see Party).

Food 9, Service 8, Atmosphere 7

GQ, Kommendörsgatan 23, Östermalm

Tel: 08 5456 7430   www.gqrestaurang.se
Open: 5.30–11.30pm. Closed Sundays.   690kr
International

The name GQ is nothing to do with the magazine, but is meant to denote
Gastronomic Intelligence, in much the same way that IQ denotes intellectual

cleverness. It has all the things you'd expect of a chic Stockholm restaurant – a location in swanky Östermalm, interior décor based on a neutral colour palette enlivened by pieces of modern art, and polished, attentive service. But the big surprise is the food philosophy. The chef, Jürgen Grossmann, is a proponent of the idea that you can eat wisely and indulgently at the same time. So while the meal is undoubtedly delicious, it's also extremely healthy. Expect dishes like Wagyu beef with green papaya, broccoli, ox tongue and truffle vinaigrette, or grilled monkfish with beans and pak choi. The chef has achieved a sort of culinary holy grail: guilt-free gourmet food.

Food 8, Service 8, Atmosphere 7

Halv Grek Plus Turk, Jungfrugatan 33, Östermalm

Tel: 08 665 9422   www.halvgrekplusturk.se
Open: daily, 5.30pm–midnight   460kr
Greek/Turkish

Halv Grek Plus Turk, as you might guess, combines Greek and Turkish cuisine. The result is a juxtaposition of the traditional with the innovative and exotic, and a reputation that makes booking essential, particularly at weekends. Eastern Mediterranean décor is achieved with mirror-encrusted cushions and bright blue finishes on walls and furniture, giving the main restaurant the feel of a Greek island. Next door, there is a small bar with light-blue mosaic tiles covering the walls and lighting provided by Moroccan-inspired shades and lanterns. It's worth going in just for a cocktail, but the food deserves plenty of attention, too. This place is interesting from every angle, and this includes the diverse crowd, all of whom are here to eat

something less ordinary than the continental 'cross-over' fare offered in so many of Stockholm's restaurants.

Food 7, Service 7, Atmosphere 8

Kungsholmen, Norr Mälarstrand, Kajplats 464, Kungsholmen

Tel: 08 5052 4450 www.kungsholmen.com
Open: 5pm–1am. Closed Sundays.   670kr
International

Kungsholmen is the name of both the restaurant and the island on which it stands. It's located a short walk past the City Hall (Stadshuset). A sibling to Fredsgatan 12, it's a new concept in dining for the city: a super-fashionable 160-seat food hall where people order their dinner from different food stations. There's a bread bar, pasta bar, sushi bar, salad bar, soup bar, bistro bar,

grill bar and, to finish off, an ice-cream bar. The concept is good fun, and the restaurant always buzzing, but be warned that this multiple-kitchen set-up means that the dishes you and your dining companions order will invariably arrive at different times. Outside, the restaurant has its own jetty, which juts out into the harbour and is a lovely place for a drink on a summer's evening. The restaurant's cocktail menu is one of the best in town.

Food 8, Service 7, Atmosphere 7

Lux, Primusgatan 116, Lilla Essingen
Tel: 08 619 0190 www.luxstockholm.com
Open: 11.30am–2pm Tues–Fri; 5–11pm Tues–Sat   805kr
Swedish Fusion

Lux occupies a listed red-brick building that once served as the canteen for Electrolux, hence the restaurant's name. Don't be put off by its location: Lilla

Essingen is a small island close to Kungsholmen that's easily reached by bus, taxi or even on foot if you fancy a pleasant stroll. However you get there, it's worth the effort. The chef-owners, Henrik Norström and Peter Johansson, describe the food as being based on traditional Swedish cuisine but inspired by their travels. The result feels modern, inventive and, needless to say, utterly delicious. The room is very Scandinavian in appearance: modern, unpretentious, simple. In the summer be sure to request a table outside on the terrace, which has marvellous views over the water. Afterwards you can pop into Lux Dessert och Choklad, a little jewel box of a shop close to the restaurant that sells Lux's breads, chocolate and ready-made desserts.

Food 9, Service 8, Atmosphere 8

Mathias Dahlgren at the Grand Hotel, Södra Blasieholmshamnen 6, Östermalm

Tel: 08 679 3584 www.mdghs.com
Open: noon–2pm Mon–Fri; 6pm–midnight Mon–Sat (Matbaren); 7pm–midnight Mon–Sat (Matsalen)
Matbaren 800kr, Matsalen 1150kr

Scandinavian

Since it opened in 2007, Mathias Dahlgren's restaurant in the Grand Hotel has been collecting rave reviews. One Swedish newspaper, *Svenska*

Dagbladet, gave it 6 out of 6 points. Another, *Dagens Industri*, awarded it 24 points out of a possible 25, the highest rating in the whole country, and Michelin awarded it one star . We see no reason to disagree. It is simply outstanding. There are two rooms with two distinct personalities. The Matbaren (Food Bar) is more casual, with wooden chairs and tables, a tiled floor, and stainless steel bar. It's also more affordable than the Matsalen, which is classically elegant. Unlike his last restaurant, Bon Lloc, which had a Catalan name and a Latin-influenced menu, this new venture is totally Scandinavian. Reservations are taken up to a month in advance. If it's fully booked, you can sometimes find space to sit at the Matbaren's bar. In the Matsalen, request the table for two in the window overlooking the Royal Palace.

Food 10, Service 10, Atmosphere 10

Operahuset, Karl XII's Torg, Norrmalm

Tel: 08 676 5809 www.operakallaren.se
Open: See web. Operakällaren 1670kr Operabaren 815kr Bakfickan 730kr
International

In addition to staging ballets and operas, the Opera House offers several excellent places to eat. Operakällaren is the most lavish, romantic and expensive, with plenty of gilt and oil paintings on the wall. Café Opera is the most fashionable; after dinner it gradually transforms into the city's poshest nightclub (see Party). But the two most likeable spots are Bakfickan and Operabaren. Bakfickan (The Back Pocket) has bags of charm, with its dark-green lampshades, marble counter, and white tile walls smothered with framed photographs from past productions.

It attracts local business execs at lunchtime and pre- and post-theatre diners at night. Operabaren is similarly relaxed and should not to be missed by a visitor to Stockholm. Opened in 1905, it's decorated in Jugendstil, the Scandinavian version of art nouveau. To sit in this beautiful room with meatballs and a Swedish beer is a marvellous experience.

Food 8, Service 7, Atmosphere 9

PA & Co, Riddargatan 8, Östermalm

Tel: 08 611 0845
Open: 5pm–midnight daily   580kr
Swedish

PA & Co has something of a reputation for being popular with the artistic community – actors, writers, artists – and you'll often spot the occasional celebrity dining here. Despite this and the fact that it's very close to Stureplan, the heart of fashionable Stockholm, PA & Co remains determinedly unpretentious. Stockholm regulars make up the majority of the crowd and they come to enjoy the good food and relaxed atmosphere.

Nothing about the place, neither the food nor the interior, is at all fancy. Seen from the outside the place looks a bit scruffy. But don't be put off. It's one of the most consistently enjoyable places to dine in the city and pulls in an interesting crowd. Although they don't take advance reservations, if you call for a table the same evening they'll usually hold a space for you.

Food 8, Service 7, Atmosphere 8

Peacock Dinner Club, Tegnérgatan 37, Vasastan

Tel: 08 790 0020 www.peacockdinnerclub.com   500kr
Open: 6pm (4pm Fri)–1am (3am Thurs–Sat). Closed Sundays and Mondays.
Asian

The first Peacock Dinner Club opened in Sweden's second city, Gothenburg. Now it has come to Stockholm, to the delight of anyone want-

ing a great plate of tempura, sashimi and some sublime wontons, or just a late drink in lovely surroundings. The décor is stunning, with subdued lighting that gradually shifts colour, carpeting emblazoned with images of peacock feathers, and sleek seating upholstered in golden fabric. The kitchen is open until 11pm, after which the club functions as a late night lounge. No one under 23 is allowed in, which ensures a more mature crowd. And because it's located away from most other late-night places, it's not plagued with ultra-fashionable patrons. The food is so good you should go for dinner, but the atmosphere and cocktails mean that you'll probably want to stay until closing time.

Food 7, Service 7, Atmosphere 7

Pontus!, Brunnsgatan 1, Östermalm

Tel: 08 5452 7300   www.pontusfrithiof.com
Open: 11.30am–1am Mon–Fri; 1pm–1am Sat   645kr
Eclectic

Pontus! opened in the summer of 2007 and it's fair to say it has earned that exclamation mark. There's nothing else quite like it in Stockholm. Named after its owner, Pontus Frithiof, it's an establishment of many parts. There's a

cocktail bar, a dim sum station, a sushi bar and, tucked away near the entrance, a very cosy oysters-and-champagne bar. Then there's the main restaurant on the lower level, which is stunningly decorated with specially commissioned wallpaper that gives the illusion of dining surrounded by shelves laden with books (everything from *The Dangerous Book for Boys* to *Death in Venice* and Pontus's own cookbook). Thankfully, the food more than matches the hype. At the weekend there's a DJ on hand, but weekday nights see lots of local office workers dropping in for a drink on their way home.

Food 7, Service 7, Atmosphere 8

Portofino Brännkyrkagatan 93, Södermalm
Tel: 08 720 3550 www.portofino.nu
Open: 5pm–midnight Mon–Sat   510kr
Italian

When pop star Beyoncé is spotted coming out of an Italian restaurant located on a rather ordinary street in Södermalm, you know that something special is going on inside that kitchen. Portofino seemed to emerge from nowhere to become one of the new stars of the Stockholm dining scene. Certainly its location and appearance give little indication of just how good the food is. Peer in the window and it looks like any other Italian restaurant, and the menu sticks to the expected dishes: veal carpaccio, mushroom cannelloni, panna cotta, tiramisu. But the prices are fair and its success has been driven by word of mouth, rather than any cunning PR strategy. People ate here, loved it, and urged their friends to visit. It's as simple, and as wonderful, as that.

Food 8, Service 7, Atmosphere 6

Prinsen, Mäster Samuelsgatan 4, Östermalm
Tel: 08 611 1311 www.restaurangprinsen.se   675kr
Open: 11.30am–11.30pm Mon–Fri; 1–11.30pm Sat; 5–10.30pm Sun
Scandinavian

This city centre bistro is one of the gems of the town. It's been serving
everything from scampi and shrimp salad to the classic Biff Rydberg since
1897. Its history is evident the minute you step inside. You'll find banquettes
covered in cognac-coloured leather, gleaming wooden panelling, and waiters
dressed in starched white uniforms (some of them seem to have been there
as long as the restaurant itself). The food is mostly traditionally Scandinavian,

with some French influences. A plate of Toast Pelle Jansson (raw fillet of
beef, whitebait roe and red onion) makes a perfect lunchtime snack to ener-
gize you for further shopping on nearby Birger Jarlsgatan. In keeping with its
old-fashioned style the service is exemplary, if slightly formal. In the summer
the sidewalk dining is particularly popular.

Food 7, Service 8, Atmosphere 8

Le Rouge, Brunnsgränd 2–4, Gamla Stan
Tel: 08 5052 4430 www.lerouge.se
Open: 5pm–1am. Closed Sundays.   820kr
French

The owners of Le Rouge have a good track record, having previously made
great successes of Kungsholmen (see page 64), Fredsgatan 12 (see page 62)
and several other restaurants. Their newest venture is perhaps their most

opulent, looking like something from *fin de siècle* Paris: a 125-seat cellar restaurant that's adorned with an abundance of scarlet fabric and with seats upholstered in rich red velvet. It's all very Moulin Rouge, with a decadent French menu to match. There's also Le Bar Rouge, where you can have lunch or drop in for cocktails. (Note that the bar opens onto Österlång-gatan while the restaurant is reached from Brunnsgränd, around the corner.) Too many Stockholm restaurants opt for modern Swedish minimalism, with white walls and an absence of ornamentation. Le Rouge triumphs by daring to be richer, redder and a lot more fun.

Food 8, Service 7, Atmosphere 8

Sturehof, Stureplan 2, Östermalm
Tel: 08 440 5730   www.sturehof.com
Open: 11am–2am Mon–Fri; noon–2am Sat; 1pm–2am Sun   760kr
Swedish

Sturehof is always open and always busy, but it's also so big that you can usually get a table if you're happy to wait a while in the white-tiled bar. It has been in business for well over a century, and the reasons for its success are easy to see. Its location on Stureplan is perfect, the jacket-wearing wait-ers know their stuff, and the traditional Swedish food rarely disappoints. It can be particularly enjoyable to come here on those days – like Christmas, New Year's Day, or just an average Sunday – when the rest of the city seems to be deserted. It's the sort of place that Stockholmers like to go to for a meal with their family, so you'll often see several generations at the same

table. A traditional place for traditional food.

Food 7, Service 7, Atmosphere 8

Teatergrillen, Nybrogatan 3, Östermalm
Tel: 08 5450 3562 www.teatergrillen.se
Open: 11.30am–2.30pm Mon–Fri; 5pm–1am Tues–Sat   980kr
International

This is part of a family of restaurants that also includes its immediate neighbour, the glamorous bar-restaurant Riche (see Drink) and Sturehof (above).
Teatergrillen lives up to its name in terms of location, clientele and design.
With the entrance close to the Dramaten theatre, the restaurant attracts
enthusiastic theatre-goers and artistic types who appreciate the theatrical
interior. Masks hang on the walls above intimate niches upholstered in a

shocking red. The food is excellent – with lots of lobster, oysters and other luxurious items – with prices that suit the wallets of the sort of diners who wouldn't dream of booking the cheap seats for a matinee. Many dishes are named after actors and if you want to really be theatrical, you can book what was once Ingmar Bergman's private table.

Food 7, Service 7, Atmosphere 8

Vassa Eggen, Birger Jarlsgatan 29, Östermalm
Tel: 80 216 169 www.vassaeggen.com   850kr
Open: 11.30am–2pm, 6–11pm (10pm Mon). Closed Sat lunch and Sun.
Mediterranean

Vassa Eggen has been one of the most popular places to dine in the centre

of town since it opened in 1999. Its success is a result of the combination of a prime location on Birger Jarlsgatan, inventive modern cooking with a hint of a Mediterranean accent, excellent waiters who know their stuff and an extremely cool décor. At lunchtime it's popular with the expense account crowd, but in the evening it attracts a more varied clientele. By the way, the restaurant's name, 'The Sharp Edge', is taken from the W. Somerset Maugham novel known in English as *The Razor's Edge*. In 2007, the owners opened a terrific deli-style café just across the road called

Albert and Jack's (Engelbrektsgatan 3). It bakes all its breads on the premises and is perfect if you would prefer an easy-but-excellent lunch on the go rather than fine dining at the parent restaurant.

Food 8, Service 8, Atmosphere 8

Wedholms Fisk, Nybrokajen 17, Östermalm

Tel: 08 611 7874 www.wedholmsfisk.se   975kr

Open: 11.30am–2pm, 6–11pm Mon; 11.30am–11pm Tues–Fri; 5–11pm Sat

Seafood

As you'd expect in a city surrounded by water, there's no end of seriously good seafood on offer in Stockholm. That said, Wedholms Fisk is still in a

league of it own. Decorated with plain wooden tables and soft grey walls, the interior is elegant, simple and quintessentially Swedish. The same could be said of the menu. Here the philosophy is that nothing should overshadow the quality of the fish. Many dishes feature fish that has simply been grilled, fried or poached, and is then served with some vegetable and maybe a little sauce on the side. Nothing fussy and nothing fancy. (Nothing cheap either, but that's to be expected.) On a summer's day you can sit outside and take in the views of the waterfront, but it's a pleasure to visit at any time of year. If the dining room is busy, you can often find space in the bar, which has a separate menu.

Food 9, Service 7, Atmosphere 8

drink...

In an edition of *The New Yorker* published on 20th February 1954, a writer described a visit to Stockholm. The picture he painted was a bleak one. Bars and nightclubs were forbidden by law. Alcohol could only be served in restaurants, and only when food was ordered. To get around this, many places kept a tired, stale sandwich on hand that could be brought to the table as an excuse to get a glass of wine or beer. The sandwich wasn't eaten, but was re-served to other thirsty guests who were more interested in drinking than eating. On reaching the age of 25, a man could apply for a ration book that allowed him to buy up to three litres of liquor a month from the state alcohol monopoly. Married women weren't allowed to buy their own booze at all, and while single women were permitted to have up to a litre a month, they were generally discouraged from doing so.

How times have changed – though not entirely beyond recognition. There's still a small but vocal temperance lobby in Sweden, alcohol is still controlled by a

state monopoly (Systembolaget), and most bars still serve food. But today those bars are generally friendly and inviting, no stale sandwich is required, and the single women of Sweden are free to drink to their hearts' content.

Some of the more central venues in Stockholm, particularly those around Stureplan, are lively every night of the week. However, many Stockholmers tend to be quite abstemious during the week and then go wild at the weekends, when bars generally don't close their doors until 2am. To make a

very broad generalization, to which there are many exceptions, the bars in Östermalm tend to be a bit posher while those on Södermalm have a more laid-back vibe.

When they do go out, most locals tend to stick to drinking beer and wine (rosé is virtually compulsory in the summer) but Stockholm is at last developing a cocktail culture. This is due in part to a growing number of bartenders who know their drinks and can mix expert cocktails with ease. Places like Gondolen, Kunghsholmen and Pontus! pride themselves on the calibre of their cocktails and the finesse of their bartenders.

In other cities around the world bars, restaurants and clubs are very different creatures. In Stockholm, it's sometimes hard to tell them apart. At most of the places listed in this chapter you can get something to eat, and at some of them you could get a fantastic three-course dinner and then spend the night dancing.

Wherever you go, take a well-loaded wallet because drinks don't come cheap. A beer will set you back around 45kr, a glass of wine starts at around 65kr, and cocktails cost upwards of 90kr. There's no need to tip your bartender with each drink, but if your change is just a few coins it's considered good form to leave them on the bar.

Six of the best:
• The Cadier Bar, for a sunset view of the Royal Palace.
• Mälarpaviljongen, for a summer night's drink on the floating bar.
• Pontus!, for cocktails and a side order of dim sum.
• Riche, for champagne with affluent Stockholmers.
• Och Himlen Därtill, for the most stupendous view in the city.
• Inferno, for drinks in August Strindberg's house.

Absolut Ice Bar, Nordic Sea Hotel, Vasaplan 4, Norrmalm
Tel: 08 505 63000   www.nordicseahotel.se
Open: 4.30pm–midnight Mon–Fri; 3pm–midnight Sat–Sun

By now, who hasn't heard of Sweden's Ice Hotel? Well, when this bar opened it was the world's first ice bar (several more have since been

launched). Situated in the lobby of the Nordic Sea (see Sleep), the Ice Bar is the hotel's star attraction and, unsurprisingly, draws in quite a few tourists. While drinking in a room where the temperature is minus 5° Celsius might not be everyone's idea of fun, it makes a change from the average watering-hole. Fur-lined coats and warm boots are provided for customers before they venture in to sample the only alcohol available – Absolut vodka served in glasses made from ice. The ice is imported from the north of Sweden and comes from the same source as that of the Ice Hotel. You need a ticket to get in and because it is so popular you should book ahead. Tickets include one drink, and give you 45 minutes of frosty drinking time.

Allmänna Galleriet 925, Kronobergsgatan 37, Kungsholmen
Tel: 08 410 68100   www.ag925.se
Open: 5–11pm Tues; 5pm–1am Weds–Sat

It doesn't harm AG925's popularity that it can be tricky to find. Housed in a former silver workshop (the 925 in its name refers to the number that denotes sterling silver), it's hidden away behind an unmarked door next to a porn shop on a nondescript street on Kungsholmen. When it first opened its popularity was helped by the fact that its location felt like an insider secret. The interior has retained a stark, warehouse-like atmosphere with

concrete floors and white-tiled walls. The sofas are ideal to lounge on for a few hours, watching fashionable Stockholmers come and go. There's often a DJ, but the music never drowns out conversation, and the owners organize regular art exhibitions. It's lively most evenings with the after-work crowd, but it also has an excellent, relaxed restaurant that pulls in the patrons.

Cadier Bar, Grand Hotel, Södra Blasieholmshamnen 8, Östermalm

Tel: 08 679 3585   www.grandhotel.se
Open: daily, 7am–2am (1am Sun)

A few years ago the Cadier Bar was distinctly underwhelming. A fairly ordinary hotel bar with – the horror! – a television hanging overhead. Then it

closed for renovation and re-emerged as quite simply one of the most beautiful bars in the country. Service is friendly, attentive and not the least bit snobbish. The room, with its polished woodwork and sparkling crystal light fixtures, gleams. Purple upholstery adds a regal touch but the crowd is surprisingly mixed – hotel guests, local office staff having an 'afterwork' (as the Swedes call it), out-of-towners who've popped into the city for a night out. Go early to grab a seat by the window with a perfect view of the Royal Palace and order a glass of champagne. While there's no dress code as such, the smarter you look the more at home you'll feel.

Gondolen, Stadsgården 6, Södermalm

Tel: 08 641 7090 www.gondolen.se
Open: 11.30am (4pm Sat)–1am. Closed Sundays.

If you're new to the city, Gondolen is the perfect place for a first drink – so long as you get there before sunset. It hangs underneath a viewing platform on the edge of Södermalm, close to Gamla Stan, and has the second-best

views in the city (Och Himlen Därtill is the winner). It's easy to spot Gondolen – looking across from the Old Town you'll see several neon signs and an illuminated clock on its exterior – but it can be tricky to reach. The entrance is tucked away beside the McDonald's. Don't take the lift to the viewing platform itself. In addition to the panoramic view, Gondolen has a deserved reputation for mixing excellent cocktails. Come early if you want to be sure of a seat by the window. Alternatively, make an evening of it and dine in the restaurant, which is a sibling to Eriks Bakficka (see Eat).

Grodan, Grev Turegatan 16, Östermalm

Tel: 08 679 6100 www.grodan.se

Open: 11.30am–1am (3am Fri/Sat) Mon–Sat; 1pm–midnight Sun

'The Frog' is one of Stockholm's most consistently fashionable hang-outs and one of the most bustling meeting places for the fashionable folks of Östermalm. This is due in large part to its location on Grev Turegatan, a shopping street that serves as one of the main arteries of this part of town.

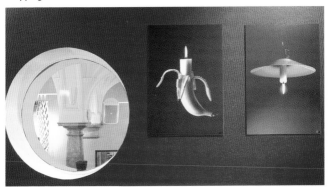

Grodan is also known for its restaurant, which in stark contrast to the minimalist bar is in a room that looks as if it's not been touched for centuries and is covered with original murals and ornate decorations. There's also the Cocktail Club (see Party), another rendezvous point for the Östermalm elite. If you can snag one of the outdoor tables in the summer, or a window seat at any time of year, the people watching is unrivalled, particularly at the weekend. However, unless you turn up early, it's usually standing-room only.

Inferno, Drottninggatan 85, Norrmalm/Vasastan

Tel: 08 201 650 www.barinferno.se

Open: 4pm–midnight (1am Thurs–Sat). Closed Sundays.

You expect a degree of drama at Inferno. After all, this is the building that August Strindberg called home towards the end of his life. A bust of the writer stares down from a shelf just above the Scotch whiskies. Many of the cocktails take their name from his works: the Miss Julie, for instance, which

is made with Champagne, strawberries and vanilla. The bar takes its named from a book Strindberg wrote following his so-called Inferno period, but the experience of visiting is far from infernal. In fact, it's heavenly. This is one of the best places in the city. The long, narrow bar is simply furnished in black and white but with blood red lighting that lends an air of the theatrical. Other bars may be bigger or louder or more fashionable, but Inferno's success is built on excellent food and drink provided by friendly staff in a cosy, compact space that quickly foster a great atmosphere.

Kungsholmen, Norr Mälarstrand, Kajplats 464, Kungsholmen

Tel: 08 505 24450 www.kungsholmen.com
Open: 5pm–1am. Closed Sundays.

The name is a little confusing: it's called Kungsholmen and it's on

Kungsholmen. Known primarily as one of the most fashionable restaurants in the city, and a sibling to Fredsgatan 12 (see Eat) it also has a busy bar scene. The cocktail list is splendid. It lists drinks by region of origin – North America, Europe, Middle East, etc. – and then offers both classic and contemporary options. For something Asian, for instance, you might choose a modern Lychee Martini or a good old-fashioned Singapore Sling, while North America is represented by the new-fangled Pumpkin Punch or the traditional Sazerac. During the summer, a bar opens on a floating pontoon moored in front of the restaurant. On warm days, it's very popular so if you get here and it's too busy, head along to Mälarpaviljongen, which also has a bar on the water.

Lokal, Scheelegatan 8, Kungsholmen

Tel: 08 650 9809 www.lokallemon.com
Open: daily, 4pm–1am (3am Fri–Sat)

Lokal is just one of several restaurant-bars on Scheelegatan, but it's one of the best. The interior is trendy, but not painfully so – and the same could be

said of the clientele. The room is dominated by the long, curved bar, which is lined each night by a pleasant crowd of young professionals. You could come for dinner, but the bar is the heart of the place. Besides, because Scheelegatan is one of Stockholm's most restaurant-packed streets, it's more fun to drop into Lokal for a drink (they make a mean mojito) and then just see what sort of cuisine you feel like eating. There's often a DJ playing and at the weekend it can get crowded. The bar's sibling and neighbour, Lemon, is another good choice for a drink with a similarly vibe. Neither venue is overly flash, but both are friendly and reliable.

Mården, Tulegatan 24, Vasastan
Tel: 08 612 6550 www.marden.se
Open: 5pm–midnight (1am Thurs–Sat). Closed Sundays and Mondays.

Mården has a lengthy drinks list, and a reputation for making cocktails very well indeed. House specials include the Rhubarb (Cuban rum, rhubarb purée, vanilla, lemon) and the Absolutely Crushed (Absolut Citron, kumquats and passion fruit). As a result, Mården is always an attractive proposition. It's located just a few minutes from Storstad, and is most popular at weekends for start-of-the-evening drinks, before the crowd moves on

in search of somewhere to dance. The atmosphere, décor and service are resolutely unpretentious. The building was previously a pharmacy and follows the Swedish habit of naming pharmacies after animals – in this case, a pine martin. If too many lemongrass martinis or frozen daiquiris reduce your desire to walk through Vasastan in search of dinner, Mården's continental cuisine is delicious. If you don't want a full meal, you can always snack from the excellent bar menu.

Mälarpaviljongen, Norr Mälarstrand 64, Kungsholmen
Tel: 08 650 8701 www.malarpaviljongen.se
Open: daily, 11am–midnight April–September

If it's a sunny day – or better yet, a warm night – then Mälarpaviljongen can be sublime. Even on chillier days, when patrons use the blankets provided to stay warm, this outdoor café-bar can be great fun. Located on the southern edge of Kungsholmen, it's got good food (including excellent cakes and pas-

tries) and great views over the water. Its only failing is exasperatingly slow service. During the summer, it's almost always hopping. By day, everyone comes here, from mothers with prams to elderly couples out for an afternoon stroll. Then as the hour gets later, and the DJs start playing, the crowd gets younger, cooler and gayer (though in Stockholm no one really cares one way or the other). In summer 2007 a huge floating deck was added. Stepping onto it feels like you're stepping onto a yacht. When the weather is good, Mälarpaviljongen should not be missed.

Nox, Grev Turegatan 30, Östermalm

Tel: 08 545 82400 www.nox.se
Open: 5pm–1am Tues–Thurs; 4pm–1am Fri; 6pm–1am Sat

With its black walls, black-clad staff, black leather sofas and smooth

concrete floors, Nox could be dropped into any major city in the world and immediately grab the attention and patronage of a suitably fashionable black-clad crowd. It's certainly one of the more self-consciously stylish bars in Stockholm, and further enhances Grev Turegatan's reputation as one of the hippest streets for food and drink. The bar area is upstairs while food is served downstairs. The food menu is short and simple, and won't surprise anyone who spends some time in Stockholm. The dishes on offer – beef 'Rydberg', tuna fish with Thai vegetables, tiger prawns with tagliatelle – are the sort of things you'll find at many bars, but they're expertly done. Best of all, when it's warm enough they open a large outdoor lounge in the inner courtyard of the building.

Och Himlen Därtill, Götgatan 78, Södermalm
Tel: 08 660 6068 www.restauranghimlen.se
Open: 6pm–1am Mon–Thurs; 5pm–3am Fri; 6pm–3am Sat

The name roughly translates as 'And Heaven Above' and refers to the fact

that this is Stockholm's highest bar, located on the 26th floor of a skyscraper on Södermalm. The drinks are expensive (85kr for a glass of white wine; 138kr for a cocktail), the décor is unremarkable, the bar staff wear silly red braces, it's often too crowded… and yet none of that matters one jot as you stare out of the floor-to-ceiling windows. You can see the entire city in all directions and because the bar is dimly lit, with soft pink lighting that pre-sumably reduces reflections on the glass, you feels as if there's nothing between you and world outside. It is, in short, a staggering experience that should be avoided by anyone with a fear of heights but experienced by everybody else. Rather than battling the crowd at the bar, you can reserve a table for a drink. Alternatively, dine in the restaurant which is one floor beneath the bar.

Pelikan, Blekingegatan 40, Södermalm
Tel: 08 556 09090 www.pelikan.se
Open: 4pm–midnight Mon–Thurs; 1pm–1am Fri–Sat; 1pm–midnight Sun

Stockholm is full of super fashionable places to go for a drink, but there are some nights when you don't want anything fashionable. Instead, you would prefer something completely traditional. Instead of yet more white-walled Swedish minimalism, there are times you want something in a century-old room that's furnished with plain wooden tables, a tiled floor, and murals of

monkeys clambering up huge columns. And it's on nights like these that you should head to Pelikan. It's one of the few old-fashioned beer halls still in existence in the city and it attracts a friendly, boisterous crowd who don't care what label you're wearing. If you happen to get hungry, the food on offer suits the setting. The menu is all about *husmanskost* – traditional Swedish cooking that's heavy on the meat and potatoes – which is just what you need after a few beers.

Pontus!, Brunnsgatan 1, Östermalm

Tel: 08 545 27300   www.pontusfrithiof.com
Open: 11.30am–1am Mon–Fri; 1pm–1am Sat

Pontus!, which is named after its owner, Pontus Frithiof, opened near Stureplan in the summer of 2007 and since then it's built a reputation for outstanding food and some of the best cocktails in the whole of Scandinavia. The cocktail list is excellent. The Thai Mojito and the Jerry Thomas Breakfast Manhattan – a blend of whisky, orange curaçao and English marmalade – are particularly wonderful. It's a huge place spread over three levels. Just inside

the entrance there's a small champagne-and-oysters bar, while the main bar is attached to a sushi bar and a dim sum station that sends up great clouds of steam. The restaurant, downstairs, is decorated with custom-made wallpaper that creates the illusion of dining in some outlandish library where the walls are smothered with outsized books. It's a popular destination for office executives every weeknight, with DJs playing at the weekend.

Riche, Birger Jarlsgatan 4, Östermalm

Tel: 08 545 03560   www.riche.se
Open: 11.30–midnight (1am Tues, 2am Weds–Fri); noon–2am Sat

There's nothing nouveau about this Riche. This restaurant and bar has been here since 1893, reputedly modelled after the Café Riche in Paris. However the name is entirely appropriate. Every evening you'll hear the steady pop-pop-pop of Champagne bottles being opened for a distinctly affluent crowd of Stockholmers including the occasional Swedish celeb. Its location at the

head of Birger Jarlsgatan, just a short walk from Stureplan, makes it an ideal starting point to meet friends before a night out hopping from bar to bar. Riche gets busy from the minute people start to leave work and later in the evening there's usually a bouncer on the door to keep the crush inside manageable. The best time to visit is early evening, when you can still catch the bartender's eye to get a drink and move around with some degree of comfort. The food is great, but at some of the tables be prepared to get jostled as the crowd grows.

Soap Bar, Nybrogatan 1, Östermalm

Tel: 08 611 0021 www.soapbar.se
Open: 11am–3am Mon–Fri; noon–3am Sat; 8am–3am Sun

For more than a decade Soap Bar has been a bubbly city centre nightspot. Its popularity is helped by its proximity to Dramaten, the city's principle

theatre, so from 10.30pm you can expect a post-theatre crowd to descend and discuss the evening's performance. Not that it's a serious theatrical bar – the crowd tends to be extremely fashionable, extremely cheerful, mostly in their 20s and 30s, and very into the music being played. The relatively small interior quickly fills up and the crowd spills out onto Nybrogatan, appreciative of the bar's outdoor heat lamps on colder nights. In a city where the weekends tend to be frenetic and weekdays calm, it's nice to find a place that's often hopping during the midweek, especially one with good food and friendly staff. It's also open to 3am every night of the week.

Storstad, Odengatan 41, Vasastan
Tel: 08 673 3800 www.storstad.se
Open: 5pm–1am Mon–Thurs; 4pm–3am Fri; 6pm–3am Sat

Despite Storstad's excellent food, it's usually thought of as a watering-hole rather than a dining-spot. With its sleek interior (dark wood, brown leather, pale walls), it has a clean and sophisticated look. And on weekdays, the after-work crowd in their dark suits reinforce this impression. It's one of the main hubs of social life in Vasastan, though as the week progresses you can

expect more variety as the alternative Södermalm crowd and fashionable Östermalm drinkers venture further from home for a night on the town. The long room quickly becomes packed and guests overflow to the upstairs bar or the outdoor tables during the summer. The name 'Big City' is presumably intended to be tongue in cheek. The owners also run neighbouring Olssons Video (Odengatan 41), which looks from the outside like a sleazy sex den but is, in fact, a dimly lit but perfectly respectable bar known for its music.

Sturehof, Stureplan 2, Östermalm
Tel: 08 440 5730 www.sturehof.com
Open: 11am–2am Mon–Fri; noon–2am Sat; 1pm–2am Sun

Open since 1897, Sturehof is a Stockholm institution located slap-bang on Stureplan, the epicentre of Stockholm nightlife. In addition to its excellent

restaurant (see Eat), it has several places to grab a drink. First of all, just inside the entrance from Sturegallerian, there's a classic white-tiled bar that attracts a professional post-work crowd. Then there's another bar that's reached by walking through the restaurant. In the summer there's also a large outdoor seating area, which fills up quickly as soon as the days are warm enough. Finally, and rather surprisingly considering how starchy the restaurant can seem, there's Obaren, located at the rear of the restaurant. It regularly has live music and appeals to a younger, trendier crowd. In a city that can sometimes seem a bit sleepy, one of the best things about Sturehof is that it's open seven days a week, 365 days a year.

snack...

Welcome to Sweden! The land that mug handles forgot!

Stockholm is full of cafés where you'll be served scalding drinks in glasses or cups with no handles. You'll have to insulate your fingers using a paper napkin until the sides are cool enough to touch. This is a prime example of how Scandinavians often opt for appearance over practicality. A fact made odder when you bear in mind how much the Swedes love their coffee.

The country has one of the highest per capita rates of coffee consumption in the world. The World Resources Institute ranks them as the sixth most caffeinated country, behind Finland, Aruba, Iceland, Norway and Denmark, but well ahead of the USA (number 22) and the UK (number 45). Generally speaking, the calibre of the coffee on offer is very high, while the quality of the tea is dismal. Stockholm is a coffee city, so those who love tea will have to search out the handful of places that know how to brew properly.

Working days are regularly interspersed with coffee breaks, while weekends are often built around them. There's even a charming Swedish word, *fika*, which has no direct translation in English but means a cup of coffee enjoyed with a little snack. It's rather like the English word 'elevenses', but not so time specific.

Cafés will often serve a range of traditional Swedish cakes. These include *princesstårta*, a sponge-and-cream confection wrapped in bright green marzipan; the *mazarin*, a pastry cup filled with almond paste; and the *dammsuga*, which translates as 'vacuum cleaner', a reference to its cylindrical appearance. Every Lent brings *semla* season, when buns filled with cream, almond paste, and dusted with sugar are eaten in large quantities, sometimes in a bowl of warm milk. These buns even changed the course of Swedish history: in 1771, King Adolf Fredrik overindulged on them and promptly died.

You'll also find lots of breads flavoured with the most popular Swedish spices: cardamom (*kardemumma*) and cinnamon (*kanel*). To get the best baked goods, go to a *konditori*, one of the traditional bakery-cafés that often make all their products on the premises. They may look a little frumpy, but their baked goods are first-rate.

When it comes to café snacks, you'll tend to see the same tasty but unoriginal sandwiches everywhere – ham and cheese, turkey and cheese, mozzarella and

tomato – plus pasta salads, soups and simple warm dishes. Bear in mind that Stockholmers always take their weekday lunch at noon. Hit the cafés earlier or later if you want to avoid the crush.

There are strict laws in Sweden that govern when a café may and may not put out its outdoor seating – come to think of it, there are strict laws for every-thing in Sweden – but as soon as they are legal the sidewalk tables and chairs appear and Stockholmers flock to them. If the weather's still chilly they wrap themselves in the blankets most cafés provide until the days get warm. One way or another they get together, order a coffee, and *fika* like mad.

When you want to grab a coffee or have a light lunch, there's no end of unre-markable cafés in town, including the drab and depressingly ubiquitous Wayne's Coffee and Robert's Coffee. Here we've picked a few that have something spe-cial about them – whether it's their coffee, their character, or just their really great cakes.

Café Rival, Mariatorget 3, Södermalm

Tel: 08 5457 8925   www.rival.se

Open: 8am–8pm Mon–Thurs; 8am–7pm Fri; 9am–7pm Sat–Sun

The Rival is one of the best hotels in town, and the neighbouring café is equally popular. Despite being large, it's often full (though you can usually find some quieter space in the upper level). The weekend brunch is particularly popular. Ask for the Café Frukost: Greek yoghurt with walnuts and

honey, a large savoury scone, some slices of cheese, a boiled egg, a tube of Kalles Caviar (Swedish fish paste that you'll either love or hate), plus orange juice and tea or coffee. The best time to visit is in the summer, when you can sit outside and enjoy the view of the square, and watch the locals popping into the excellent Rival Bakery to buy loaves. One slight drawback is the glacially slow service. When it gets busy the tables quickly get cluttered with dirty dishes that the staff don't seem in any hurry to remove.

Chaikhana, Svartmangatan 23, Gamla Stan

Tel: 08 244 500   www.chaikhana.se

Open: 11am–7pm Mon–Fri; noon–6pm Sat–Sun

Hidden away on a narrow street beside the German Church, Chaikhana is an oasis in the Old Town. This small Colonial-style tea house is the only place in Gamla Stan where you can find great tea. And thanks to its location, removed from the main tourist streets, it's rarely too crowded. Here you'll find more than 200 varieties of loose-leaf tea for sale – not dreadful fruit-scented ones, but pure and blended varieties from China, India, Sri Lanka,

Vietnam, Russia and other places were chamomile is frowned upon. Each week, 10 different teas are placed on the menu and can be ordered and enjoyed in-house. We'd recommend that you also treat yourself to some of the wonderfully fluffy English scones, served with jam and cream, or one of the excellent French pastries.

Chokladfabriken, Regeringsgatan 58, Norrmalm
Tel: 08 229 110   www.chokladfabriken.com
Open: 10am–6.30pm Mon–Fri; 10am–5pm Sat

'The Chocolate Factory' was established in 1997 and has perfected the art of producing high-quality chocolate for both eating and drinking. You can also just pop in for a coffee. The sleek and streamlined interior is typically Scandinavian, much like the truffles themselves. The one on Regeringsgatan is the smaller of the company's two cafés (the larger one is over on Södermalm, where they make the products) but this is the easier one to

reach if you're in the city centre. Needless to say, the chocolates are out-standing. While you have a drink you can watch them being made on a web-cam link to the other premises. If you are in town and invited to a dinner party, a small box of something from Chokladfabriken is the perfect gift to take along with you. The larger outlet is found at: Renstiernas Gata 12, Södermalm (see photo).

Chokladkoppen & Kaffekoppen, Stortorget 20, Gamla Stan
Tel: 08 203 170
Open: 9am–10pm Mon–Fri; 9am–11pm Sat–Sun

These must surely be the most-photographed cafés in the city. Standing side-by-side on the main square of the Old Town in two enchanting build-ings – one red, the other mustard yellow – these sibling cafés attract differ-ing customers. Chokladkoppen is nominally gay, though you'd be hard pressed to guess that on days when school groups and pensioners crowd the tiny tables. As its name suggests, Chokladkoppen is famed for its hot chocolate, which is marvellous and served in a big bowl. In the winter,

Kaffekoppen's cellar is the perfect place for a cosy coffee. In the summer, both cafés set up outdoor tables that are always packed thanks to the prime location close to the Nobel Museum and overlooking the square. At both places the service can be wobbly, but the food and drinks are wonder-ful. The sandwiches and the chocolate cake, which comes with a dollop of cream, are particularly splendid.

Gooh!, Norrlandsgatan 21, Norrmalm

Tel: 08 210 850 www.gooh.se

Open: 8am–7pm Mon–Fri; 11.30am–4.30pm Sat

Don't be put off by the name, which stands for 'Get Out of Here' and also sounds like the slang pronunciation of 'great' in Swedish. It's that rarest of things, a fast-food joint with good food. The meals come in little plastic con-

tainers, like in-flight meals, which can be taken away or microwaved on the premises. They taste good, having been developed in conjunction with the head chef of Operakällaren, one of the city's best-respected restaurants. There's even a line of gourmet baby food. To be honest, some dishes miss the mark (skip the pasta dishes which don't seem to work) but the traditional Swedish meatballs with mashed potatoes and cream sauce is delicious. And at 47 kronor, including a side order of lingon berries, it's a

steal. There are several Gooh! branches in the centre, and the range is also now available in some supermarkets. Other outlets are to be found at: Grev Turegatan 15, Östermalm, and Hötorget 4, Norrmalm.

Lasse i Parken, Högalidsgatan 56, Södermalm

Tel: 08 658 3395 www.lasseiparken.se

Open: winter: 11am–5pm Sat–Sun; summer: 11am–4.30pm Tues–Sat

This is an odd little place: a wooden house dating from the 18th century on the edge of Södermalm, close to Långholmen, surrounded by trees and greenery and with its own outdoor stage. In the summertime, they put on little shows, concerts or just screen a sporting event. On a sunny summer's afternoon, Lasse is the perfect spot for a lovely afternoon tea with traditional fruit pies, served with lashings of cream or vanilla sauce, or thick

cheese sandwiches and other snacks. However, they also have a hot menu
with dishes such as pike-perch with horseradish or an entrecote with fries.

 Being out-
doors, with
plastic furni-
ture, it's a
good place to
come with
children or
pets.
Stockholmers
regard it
fondly, as you
would an eld-
erly relative

who hasn't really kept up with the times, but is, nonetheless, jolly good fun
on occasion.

Martins Gröna, Regeringsgatan 91, Norrmalm
Tel: 08 411 5850
Open: 11am–3pm Mon–Fri. Closed July.

Compared with many of the establishments listed on these pages, 'Martin's
Greens' is distinctly plain. It's a tiny place that fills up quickly every day,

 mostly
with local
office
workers. If
you do find
a space
you'll
doubtless
have to
share your
table with
other din-
ers. Only

open for lunch, the menu is restricted to two choices each day. Customers queue at a counter to collect their meal, pausing to slice themselves some of the excellent home-baked bread. It's not at all stylish, so why do we include it? Because it's one of the few vegetarian restaurants in the city. And it's just downright nice. Martin is friendly, the food is robust and hearty, and portions are large, which explains its popularity even among the carnivorous diners of Stockholm.

Mellqvist Café & Bar, Rörstrandsgatan 4, Norrmalm
Tel: 08 302 380
Open: 7am–8pm Mon–Thurs; 7am–6pm Fri; 8am–5pm Sat; 9am–5pm Sun

This tiny, classic Italian café feels like a little corner of Milan in Stockholm. It has won a devoted clientele thanks to the quality of its coffee and its char-

acter. You don't come here to linger over a drink and work on your laptop; it's more the place for a quick coffee fix. Squeeze in when you want a well-made espresso and, perhaps, a *ciabatta* or plate of *tramezzini* to snack on. That's if there's room, of course. Its popularity means it's always busy. Don't even bother trying to get in around noon, when the local office workers descend in droves, but at other times you can usually find space to perch at the counter and quickly scan the newspapers. If you're out of luck, try one of the several other cafés on the same street, such as Xoko (see page 106).

Muffin Bakery, Fridhemsgatan 3, Kungsholmen

Tel: 08 651 8800 www.muffinbakery.se
Open: daily, 9am–6pm

The Muffin Bakery sells far more than muffins – there are assorted salads,
sandwiches and hot dishes, plus a weekend brunch plate – but the huge, glorious muffins are the real draw. The chocolate brownie and strawberry varieties are particularly good. Although there are now two city centre branch-

es of the Muffin Bakery, this one on Kungsholmen is worth knowing about
as it can serve as a useful end-point for a walk along the waterfront from
the City Hall. On a warm day you can buy some muffins and drinks and
stage an impromptu picnic in the nearby park. Alternatively, sit inside or out
at the Muffin Bakery itself, though in previous years the attentions of
crumb-hungry crows have made the outside seating resemble a scene from
The Birds. Other locations include: Tegnérgatan 11 and Drottninggatan 73,
Norrmalm.

Mälarpaviljongen, Norr Mälarstrand, Kungsholmen

Tel: 08 650 8701 www.malarpaviljongen.se
Open: daily, 11am–midnight. Closed during the winter.

Mälarpaviljongen sits right on the edge of Kungsholmen, just a short walk
from Stadshuset (City Hall). It's one of the best outdoor café-bars in town
and when the weather is right you can come here at almost any time of the
day and enjoy it, whether you want a mid-morning snack, lunch, dinner or a
late drink. Most of the tables are outside though there is one covered

room, a gazebo poking out over the water, where you can shelter in case of a sudden rain shower. In 2007 a glamorous floating deck was added, on which you can have dinner or drinks and feel as if you're on a yacht. The clientele is thoroughly mixed by day and then gets gayer as it gets later. Its only drawback is its enormous popularity. The better the weather, the harder it can be to find a table.

Non Solo Bar, Odengatan 34, Norrmalm
Tel: 08 440 2082 www.nonsolobar.com
Open: 8am–10pm Mon–Thurs; 8am–11pm Fri; 9am–11pm Sat; 10am–6pm Sun

This café-bar (which is better known as a café than a bar) has built a loyal following among young professional Stockholmers. It has a reputation for serving some of the best coffee in the city – in part because that is its declared aim. The trio who own it are former customers and passionate coffee connoisseurs who

loved the place so much that when they got the chance to buy it they did. While the calibre of the coffee has remained the primary selling point, you can also just come for a glass of wine and a plate of very affordable pasta for lunch or dinner, maybe with a glass of *grappa* as a chaser in a nod to the café's Italian style. During the summer months the outdoor seating at Odengatan is always packed.

Riddarbageriet, Riddargatan 18, Östermalm
Tel: 08 660 3375
Open: 8am–6pm (3pm Sat). Closed Sundays.

This little café-bakery is an Atkins dieter's nightmare. It's known for having the best bread in the city. This bread is also sold at the Rival Bakery, which adjoins the Rival Hotel on Södermalm. There are dozens of different varieties, as well as lots of exquisite cakes. The Catalan – delicate little tarts

made from ground almonds with a layer of raspberry – are particularly wonderful, as are the *bulle*, which are sweet bread buns sometimes filled with vanilla cream. Riddarbageriet is a pleasant place for lunch or *fika*, not least because it is one of the few places in town to serve tea in a teapot. Unfortunately, there are only five small marble-topped tables inside, which tend to fill up quickly and are best avoided during the lunchtime rush. But because it's not on a busy pedestrian street you can often be lucky and score a table at Riddarbageriet.

Rosendals Trädgård, Rosendalsterrassen 12, Djurgården

Tel: 08 5458 1270 www.rosendalstradgard.com

Open: daily, 11am–4pm, but check website for details, which can vary. Open
February to September.

Right in the middle of Djurgården, the island that is to Stockholm what
Central Park is to Manhattan, you'll find Rosendals Trädgård. It's a beautiful

plant nursery and café where
you come to eat organic food
and home-baked cakes sur-
rounded by flowers and trees.
On colder days lunch is served
in the greenhouses. Afterwards
feel free to stock up on potted
plants or have a whip around
the cutting garden with a pair
of scissors and go home with a
bunch of freshly cut flowers.
The on-site shop sells lots of
great organic foods and freshly
baked bread. This is an excellent destination following a
Djurgården stroll, and particularly good to visit with children, who are free to race
around the apple orchard while
their parents have a chat and a
bite to eat. Despite being only a short walk from the centre of town, you
feel like you're in the heart of the Swedish countryside.

Saluhall, Östermalmstorg, Östermalm

www.saluhallen.com

Open: daily, 9.30am–6pm (6.30pm Fri)

Unlike the other listings in this section, this isn't a single business but a collection of many. This vibrant indoor market housed in a redbrick building
dating from 1888 has several excellent places to eat at, surrounded by the
bustle of the market. For a salad and a glass of wine, visit Tysta Mari (08 667

5854). For seafood, try Gerdas (08 553 40440; www.gerdas.se) and Lisa Elmqvist (08 553 40400; www.lisaelmqvist.se), which are both utterly wonderful. There's also an outdoor branch of Lisa Elmqvist on the square outside the hall called Lisa på Torget. Nybroe Smørrebrød (08 662 2320; www.nybroe.se) serves traditional Danish open sandwiches, of which each one is a little work of art. If you can't decide which to choose just opt for the Dagens Tre, a selection of three sandwiches that changes daily.

Saturnas, Eriksbergsgatan 6, Östermalm
Tel: 08 611 7700   www.cafesaturnas.se
Open: 8am–8pm Mon–Fri; 10am–7pm Sat–Sun

Saturnas is, quite simply, Stockholm's best café. The staff is friendly. The coffee is delicious. The hot chocolate is made with melted Valrhona. The owners understand the importance of running a café with a soul. It's always bustling, but big enough so that tables open up regularly. It has newspapers to read, including the *Financial Times* and *International Herald Tribune*. And the food is fantastic. Everything is made on site, and while the sandwiches (grilled or plain) and salads are delicious, it's the French-accented cakes and desserts you'll remember: *millefeuille*, *mousse au chocolat*, *tarte rhubarbe*, *gâteau à la carotte*, a cheesecake so light it virtually floats… Their *bulle*, traditional Swedish buns flavoured with cinnamon or cardamom, have been declared the best in the city by a local newspaper. They're certainly the largest, each one the size of a small loaf. Saturnas does exactly what a café

should do: it provides you with excellent food and drink and lively company
while making you feel connected to the heartbeat of the city.

Tabac, Stora Nygatan 46, Gamla Stan
Tel: 08 101 534
Open: 10am–midnight Sun–Thurs; 11am–1am Fri–Sat

Tabac is one of the more Continental cafés in the city, offering 22 different
types of tapas as well as grilled baguettes, *bruschetta*, salads and assorted
pasta dishes. Because it's located close to Slussen, the point where you can
cross from Gamla Stan to Södermalm, it's a popular meeting place for
friends. Meanwhile, the weekday happy hour pulls in local workers as they
leave their offices. There are plenty of bad cafés in Gamla Stan that aim to
exploit visitors with substandard food and dismal service, many of them

located just one block from Tabac on Västerlånggatan, the street along which most of the tourists meander. But Tabac remains a dependable, reliable choice that's good at any time of the day or night.

Xoko, Rörstrandsgatan 15, Norrmalm

Tel: 08 318 487 www.xoko.se
Open: 7.30am–11pm (6.30pm Tues) Tues–Fri; 9am–11pm Sat; 9am–6pm Sun.
Closed Mondays.

When the man who has been responsible for the desserts at the Nobel banquets opens a café, you can expect it to be something special. Xoko is like nothing else in the city. It has a futuristic white interior illuminated by

glowing lights that gradually change colour, making it look like the sort of place Stanley Kubrick would have opened if he had gone into catering. The menu is built around the excellent desserts, though there are also sandwiches and other light meals. Here even traditional cakes are given a modern twist. On a classic *princesstårta*, for instance, the raspberries sit on top of the marzipan; at Xoko, they seemed to be bursting through it. Because Xoko is open late, is located on one of the busiest restaurant rows in the city, and has a licence to serve alcohol, many people dine nearby, then come here for dessert. No matter when you visit, it's always a treat.

Notes & Updates

party...

Some years ago, a file was bouncing around the Internet that purported to be a comparison between the club scene in a city in northern England and the nightlife of Stockholm.

The English pictures showed a frightening collection of people, some with black eyes or other disfiguring injuries, dancing drunkenly while wearing bad sportswear in dingy clubs. The Stockholm pictures, on the other hand, portrayed a glamorous world of good lighting, good fashion and good genes. While we cannot vouch for the veracity of the English snaps, the Swedish pictures seemed entirely genuine. They look, in fact, like a fairly ordinary night out in the Swedish capital.

The city's clubs are filled with the sort of blondes who would have given Hitchcock a heart attack, accompanied by tall, sexually ambiguous young men with perfect skin who look as if they've come straight from shooting an ad campaign for a new unisex cologne. Glamorous and good-looking, though not nearly as sophisticated as they appear, this breed of Stockholmer knows how to go out and have a good time.

Nights out tend to start late and go on until the early hours. People will usually stay at home or go to a bar until long after midnight before hitting the clubs. Then they dance the night away until the clubs close, some around 5am.

The club scene is concentrated around Östermalm, the smartest part of town. So in order to get in to a club, you may have to dress up a bit. Some clubs want to attract certain looks or specific types, so you need to behave accordingly and look like you deserve to be there. Also take note of varying age restrictions – most clubs adopt a 23-and-over policy but if you look the part you'll rarely be asked for ID. Arrive early to improve your chances of gaining entrance. At places such as Café Opera it's sensible to book a table and eat there first, to avoid freezing for hours in a mile-long queue outside.

For those who prefer their music live, Stockholm is less blessed. But the few music clubs are popular and filled with a genuine buzz. Fasching is the best for jazz, offering everything from funk to acid jazz and keeping the crowd going all night. Mosebacke is a famous Stockholm establishment which has, in the past, featured many of Sweden's most recognized jazz artists as well as a variety of other acts ranging from pop to classical.

Casinos in Stockholm are few and far between. The only vaguely respectable one is Casino Cosmopol, which opened in 2003, close to Fasching. Until a couple of years ago Stockholm banned casinos, and those that do now exist are governed by extremely strict laws.

2.35:1, Berns Hotel, Berzelii Park 9, Norrmalm
Tel: 08 5663 2222 www.berns.se
Open: 11pm–4am Thurs–Sun

In the past club nights regularly took over the public areas of the Berns, and occasionally still do. And when they do, they're well worth attending. The grandiose interior of the Berns makes the perfect setting for a decadent party. To stand on the balcony and watch the sunrise over Berzelii Park in the summer is always memorable. Sadly, though, the only regular club now is 2.35:1, located underneath the hotel. It's a small club, with space for only

about 200 people, and while there's a different DJ each night the general vibe is more lounge than dance club. It's known to be one of the most exclusive clubs in the city, and there's the problem: it's essentially a private members' club. Hotel guests may be able to secure entry, but it's trickier for other visitors, unless they have some very good connections to call on. The name, incidentally, is the aspect ratio of Panavision and Cinema Scope.

Café Opera, Operahuset, Kungsträdgården, Norrmalm
Tel: 08 676 5807 www.cafeopera.se
Open: 11.30–3am Mon–Sat; 1pm–3am Sun

Café Opera, located in the Opera House on Kungsträdgården, is famed as the most glamorous club in the city, at least in terms of its architecture. Unashamedly opulent, the interior is awash with glittering chandeliers and murals smother the ceiling. On a good night it also offers wall-to-wall beauty in terms of people, too. This is where Stockholm's elite – everyone from

minor royals to major footballers – comes to mingle on a Friday night. As a result, it can be tricky to get in if you just turn up outside. Instead, book a table for dinner and then simply stick around. As the night progresses, the tables are cleared away, the lights get dimmer, the music gets louder and you'll find yourself in the heart of the action.

F12 Terrassen, Fredsgatan 12, Norrmalm
Tel: 08 248 052 www.f12.se
Open: 5pm–1am Mon–Sat. Closed Sundays.

During a good Stockholm summer, when the nights are warm and light, it seems a crime to stay indoors. Thankfully, with a bit of planning you rarely have to. F12 Terrassen is an alfresco late-night lounge that takes place in conjunction with one of the city's best restaurants, Fredsgatan 12 (see Eat).

A crowd of well-dressed Stockholmers and their foreign friends cover the steps and the two terraces flanking the entrance to the Royal Academy of Fine Arts, next door to the restaurant. The sight of this grand old building illuminated with colourful lights and mobbed with people sipping drinks and enjoying the music is impressive. If you want to make a night of it, pop into the restaurant for dinner or just to graze from the bar menu before heading outside again to enjoy a little night music.

Grodan Cocktail Club, Grev Turegatan 16, Östermalm
Tel: 08 679 6100
Open: 6pm–3am Thurs–Fri; 11pm–3am Sat–Sun

One of the most striking things about the Cocktail Club located in the basement of Grodan (see Drink) is the stark contrast with the elegant gourmet restaurant upstairs. Down here the décor is almost sinful: a red glow engulfs both the main bar and the more intimate underground dens leading off it. Don't be misled by the club's name, which calls to mind genteel cocktails and perhaps a jazz trio playing. Here the music tends towards powerful techno and electronica. Come 2am, no one's too cool to not

dance. If, after a couple of hours, the ambience becomes too much of an effort, moving on won't be a problem. Situated in the middle of the Öster-malm hub of bars, there are plenty of other options just around the corner.

Hell's Kitchen, Sturegatan 4, Östermalm

Tel: 08 5450 7675 www.stureplansgruppen.se

Open: 11pm–5am Thurs–Sat

Previously known as Köket, Hell's Kitchen can be found in the basement of

Sturecompagniet (see page 116). As a result of its central location, just off Stureplan, it's one of the places where you're most likely to find yourself surrounded by other international visitors to the city (these visitors have in the past included P. Diddy and Timbaland, not to mention Swedish soccer star Freddie Ljungberg). The concept for the club is said to draw on everything from 19th-century Tokyo to ancient Rome and modern day L.A. In other words, it's a bit pretentious – but in a fun sort of way. You'll find yourself surrounded by a typical Östermalm crowd, which you'll either enjoy or find exasperating, as they tend to be highly fashionable, often attractive, and just a little bit in love with themselves.

Marie Laveau, Hornsgatan 66, Södermalm

Tel: 08 668 8500 www.marielaveau.se

Open: 5pm–midnight Tues–Weds; 5pm–3am Thurs–Sat

This is one of those outstanding Stockholm places that could just have easily been popped into the chapter on where to go for dinner or a drink. Marie Laveau is a multiple personality venue. There's a large bar at the front, with black leather sofas to lounge on, and walls that display artworks by a changing line-up of modern artists; a super cosy little bar at the back where music isn't played so you can have a decent conversation; a good, attractive

restaurant; and, at the weekend, there's the club downstairs. Because it's on Södermalm you'll get a far different crowd here than over in Östermalm. This side of town is far less self-important. The music policy varies from week to week. One night it will be all about the 80s, the next could be their celebration of Britpop known as Bangers'n'Mash. The only rules are no hip-hop and no reggae.

Obaren, Stureplan 2, Östermalm

Tel: 08 440 5730 www.sturehof.com
Open: daily, 7pm–2am

Obaren (pronounced OH-bar-en) is quite unexpected. It's an alternative music venue located at the back of Sturehof, one of the most dignified and historic of all Stockholm restaurants. By day the restaurant is the sort of place where you'll find well-heeled grandparents dining with their

grandchildren. By night, though, Obaren is home to DJs and live acts playing anything from bass-heavy hip-hop to hard rock, plus some soul and electro. The space also hosts regular art exhibitions. It has the feel of an old-school jazz club, but with an atmosphere that's just a little more pretentious. The juxtaposition of the different parts of Sturehof has a lot to recommend it. After all, there aren't many places where if you're not into the music, you can take a few steps, grab a table, and have a red-jacketed waiter bring you a plate of some of the best traditional Swedish food in town.

Patricia, Stadsgårdskajen 152, Södermalm

Tel: 08 743 0570   www.patricia.st
Open: 5pm–1am Weds–Thurs; 6pm–5am Fri–Sat; 6pm–3am Sun (gay night)

Patricia has come a long way since 1938. All the way from Middlesbrough in northern England, in fact. Since being launched this boat has worked as a

light ship in the English channel, taken part in the evacuation of Dunkirk, and served a stint as the private yacht of H.M. Queen Elizabeth, the Queen Mother. But don't expect any vestige of regal splendour. Patricia will not win any prizes for its décor, and it's far from the most sophisticated place to go out. What it is, though, is good fun. It's unpretentious, jolly and very popular. You can have dinner in the restaurant, drink at one of five restaurants (two outdoor) and hit two dance-floors. Best of all, come in the summer to take in the panoramic view of the city and watch both the sunset and the sunrise from the deck. A must for any summer visitor.

Solidaritet, Lästmakargatan 3, Östermalm

Tel: 08 678 1050 www.solidaritetstureplan.se
Open: 10pm–3am Thurs–Sat

Solidaritet is the creation of the Ahlblom family, who are the people behind
several other key nightspots in town, including Storstad (see Drink).
Solidaritet took over a space previously occupied by Halv Trappa Plus Gård,
which for a long time was one of the most popular clubs in the Östermalm

orbit. Inside there are two dance-floors and, in the middle, a large open-air
terrace. The décor is the creation of one of Sweden's best-known architecture studios, Claesson Koivisto Rune. At Solidaritet the focus is on electronic dance music, especially house and techno. Needless to say, it pulls in a
cool crowd, but the demographic of those guests skews older than in some
of the nearby clubs. It's fashionable, of course, but not painfully so.

Sturecompagniet, Sturegaten 4, Östermalm

Tel: 08 611 7800 www.stureplansgruppen.se
Open: 10pm–3am Thurs–Sat

Sturecompagniet comes from the same stable as Hell's Kitchen (see page
113) and is similarly popular with the out-of-towners. It is perhaps the best-
known nightclub in Stockholm. Certainly if you're walking past Stureplan on
a weekend night you can't fail to notice it. It has managed to retain its
pulling power, though it tends to divide public opinion. For some people it's
just too big (it's a huge place, spread over several floors), too popular and

too glitzy. Inside, the lighting and décor create a strong sense of the theatrical. Two words of warning for you: the doormen can be difficult, so be sure

to dress up and arrive early if you want to be sure of gaining access. Also, if you're over 30 you're going to feel your age when you're surrounded by the swarms of beautiful 20-somethings.

The White Room, Jakobsbergsgatan 29, Norrmalm
Tel: 08 5450 7600 www.stureplansgruppen.se
Open: 11pm–5am Weds, Fri and Sat

It's a transformation Clark Kent would be proud of. By day it's just an unassuming Espresso House coffee shop, but by night it becomes one of the smaller, cooler clubs in the city. Thev White Room comes from a family with clubbing in its blood, being a sibling of several other ventures including Hell's

Kitchen and Sturecompagniet. Separated from the rest of the family, The White Room is located a ten-minute walk from Stureplan and it's a sign of its popularity that it can lure the high-fashion crowd away from their usual stomping grounds to this less-than-fashionable street just off Regeringsgatan. The interior could hardly look more Scandinavian, furnished with ultra-modern white furniture bathed in flattering lighting. The Champagne-swilling crowd tends to be young and the music mainstream. If you want something a little more serious then head to Esque, which is just steps away (Regeringsgatan 61; 10pm–3am Fri–Sat), where you'll find the latest electronic dance music with regular guest DJs.

LIVE MUSIC

Debaser, Karl Johans Torg 1, Gamla Stan
Tel: 08 305 620 www.debaser.nu
Open: check website for details.

Located at Slussen, the point where Gamla Stan and Södermalm meet, is Debaser, one of Sweden's best smaller venues for live pop and rock. This is the place to come if you want to see up-and-coming Swedish bands, though since it opened in 2002 it's hosted everyone from Bob Dylan to The Strokes. The music policy is wide-ranging, everything from Finnish glamrock to international indie pop. Open six nights a week, there's a continual merry-go-round of club nights and concerts. Once a month there's

Svenska Musikklubben (The Swedish Music Club), which features two or three bands during the evening. Because the schedule is so packed, the best way to see what's happening is to check the website. There's also a second location, an 850-person concert venue called Medis, situated a short walk away at Medborgarplatsen on Södermalm, which features a cocktail bar overlooking the square.

Fasching Jazzclub, Kungsgatan, 63, Norrmalm
Tel: 08 5348 2960 www.fasching.se
Open: 7pm–4am Fri–Sat; 6pm–midnight Sun–Thurs

You know, as you reach the entrance of Fasching, that this is going to be everything you want a jazz club to be. It's legendary in Stockholm. Here it's all about appreciation of the music, with regular jam sessions and concerts and something happening every night of the week. Call before you go or check the website to confirm that what you want is what you're going to get, as with an eclectic music policy featuring everything from funk to Latin to soul jazz, it would be a travesty not to enjoy Fasching as much as you could. There are regular concerts from visiting artists, plus a series of club nights. Every Saturday is Club Soul, a 13-year institution. Club Rockers, a newer venture, fuses everything from 1950s rock and R'n'B

with 1970s reggae. There's also Club Mambo, which normally takes place on a Friday and focuses on Latin music, and Cuba Nocturna, a salsa club.

Mosebacke Etablissement, Mosebacke Torg 3, Södermalm
Tel: 08 5560 9890   www.mosebacke.se
Open: 5–11pm Mon–Tues; 5pm–1am Weds–Thurs; 5pm–2am Fri;
10.30am–2am Sat; 10.30am–11pm Sun

For three centuries Stockholmers have been flocking to Mosebacke for a
good night out. Today this large building on the edge of Södermalm fulfills
many roles. Some people come to eat in the restaurant (weekend brunch is
particularly popular) while others come to listen to some of the best musi-
cians in Stockholm. There's always something going on. Depending on the

night you might find jazz, pop, rock, salsa, reggae, a comedy act or an Edith
Piaf tribute show. There is also a regular line-up of club nights featuring
international DJs. The names – including Raw Fusion, Club Rub-a-Dub,
Genuine Soul Club – give you an idea of the vibe, but the website has full
details. The clientele here tends to be slightly older than over in Östermalm.
In summer the outdoor terrace offers one of the best vantage points in the
centre of town.

CASINOS

Casino Cosmopol, Kungsgatan 65, Norrmalm
Tel: 08 781 8800
Open: daily, 1pm–5am

This is Stockholm's only casino of any note. The setting is elegantly European with restored artwork and shimmering drapes hanging from the 18-foot-high ceilings. There are 30 tables and around 300 machines to play. Even though poker is enjoying a boom in Scandinavia, many of the locals are here for a bit of good old-fashioned partying rather than serious betting. If you want to make a night of it, note that Fasching (see above) is next door. Casino Cosmopol is owned by the country's largest betting company, Svenska Spel, which in turn is owned by the state of Sweden. So if you do lose all your money you can reflect on the fact that it's probably helping to prop up the social welfare system and paying for some roads and schools. Smart dress, including jackets for men, is preferred.

culture...

Huge moose, hungry wolves, a sunken ship, modern art, royal palaces, Nobel prizes, the cloak a king was murdered in, and – coming soon – lots of platform shoes and *Dancing Queen*. Stockholm's cultural life has something for everyone.

Two of the city's biggest draws are the Vasa Museet and Skansen, both of which are located on Djurgården, the greenest of the islands that make up central Stockholm. The Vasa is a 17th-century warship that sank on its maiden voyage and was salvaged from Stockholm's harbour after 334 years under the waves. Skansen is an open-air museum and zoo that shows you the history and fauna of Scandinavia. Neither place should be missed, particularly if you are visiting with children.

Other popular attractions include the Royal Palace, where you can watch the changing of the guard or tour the building and its museums; Stadshuset (also known as the City Hall), where the Nobel Banquet takes place; and the Nobel Museum.

For art lovers, there's the Moderna Museet and National Museum (right), both of which have excellent permanent collections, while Kulturhuset hosts a busy schedule of temporary exhibitions and attracts well over a million visitors each year.

Then there are many other smaller museums, including the Museum of Music, the National Maritime Museum, the Jewish Museum, the Army Museum, the Tobacco and Match Museum, the Silk Weaving Museum, the Museum of Natural History, and even the Post Museum (Sweden is, after all, the land that created the world's most valuable old stamp, the Treskilling Yellow, though so far all attempts to buy it for this museum in the Old Town have foundered).

In June 2009 the city will be gripped with Abba-mania when Abba The Museum opens, in a former tollhouse on Södermalm. The museum will tell the full story of the supergroup who were Sweden's biggest band ever. The timeline starts with Benny and Björn's first meeting and runs through to the global success of *Mamma Mia!* on stage and screen.

There are regularly sales of art and antiques at the city's auction houses – including Stockholms Auktionsverk and Auktionskompaniet – and four times a year the city's most prestigious auction house, Bukowskis, holds major sales that attract plenty of international attention. Going to the pre-sale viewing at one of these major auctions can be an experience in itself as well-to-do Stockholmers turn out in force.

The city's theatres have busy schedules for ballet, opera and drama. Occasionally you'll find performances in English, particularly at some of the smaller theatres.

With so much going on, the best way to keep in touch with what's happening is to pick up one of the newspapers. Every Thursday *Dagens Nyheter* has a supplement called *DN på Stan* (DN on the Town) which has extensive listings. For more on the city's attractions, visit the city's official tourist website: www.stockholmtown.com.

Abba The Museum, Södermalm

Tel: 08 650 0080 www.abbamuseum.com
Open: 3 June 2009

In spring 2009 Stockholm's much-anticipated Abba The Museum will open, occupying four floors of a former tollhouse on the edge of Södermalm

overlooking the harbour. The name of the museum recalls the 1977 film *Abba The Movie*. The exhibits are said to include recreations of the stage on which Abba won the Eurovision Song Contest in 1974 by singing 'Waterloo' and the helicopter from the cover of the *Arrival* album. There's also a mock-up of Polar Studios, the world-famous recording studios in which they recorded their hits. The Swedes are deservedly proud of the music of the 'Fab Fyra' Anni-Frid Lyngstad, Agnetha Fältskog, Benny Andersson and Björn Ulvaeus - and the museum looks likely to be a big hit.

Hallwylska Museet, Hamngatan 4, Norrmalm

Tel: 08 402 3000 www.hallwylskamuseet.se
Open: 11.45am (11.30am Sat/Sun)–4pm (6pm Weds). Closed Mondays.

Just down the street from NK, and opposite the Berns hotel, you'll find an extraordinary time capsule. The Hallwylska Palace was built between 1893 and 1898 and was the private home of Walther von Hallwyl, his wife

Wilhelmina and their family. They were one of the wealthiest families in the city and their house was one of the first buildings to have electricity, running water and telephones. They were also great art collectors and when they died the house and its contents, including an abundance of silver and Dutch and Flemish art, were donated to the city. And that's when time seemingly stopped inside the Palace. There are regular guided tours of the building in English offering a glimpse of how aristocratic life was lived in Stockholm at the start of the 20th century.

Kulturhuset, Sergelstorg, Norrmalm
Tel: 08 5083 1508   www.kulturhuset.stockholm.se
Opening times vary, see website

What can we say about Kulturhuset? To some, it's the vibrant cultural centre of the city, offering a packed schedule of events, including dance, film, debates, lectures, workshops, initiatives to involve young people in the arts, and even Sweden's only museum devoted to comics and graphic novels. To others, it's just a gigantic glass-fronted monolith that embodies all that is wrong with modern concepts of what culture is and its construction was an act of civic vandalism. Whether you love it or loathe it, you really can't avoid it. The building dominates Sergelstorg, a plaza in the centre of the city, and huge signs behind the façade trumpet whatever is on. Regardless of your taste, it can be worth visiting if only to have a cup of coffee in the top floor café overlooking the city.

Moderna Museet, Skeppsholmen, Östermalm
Tel: 08 5195 5200   www.modernamuseet.se
Open: 10am–6pm (8pm Tues). Closed Mondays.

Over the last 50 years the Moderna Museet (a.k.a. Modern Art Museum) has built up an impressive collection that includes pieces by Picasso, Matisse,

Miró, Duchamp and Rauschenberg. The permanent collection of paintings, photographs and sculptures is supplemented by temporary exhibitions, primarily concentrating on Nordic artists. The '1st at Moderna' series opens a new exhibition devoted to a different artist on the first day of each month. The current building, designed by Spanish architect Rafael Moneo and built in 1998, provides an appropriately contemporary home for such a magnificent collection. The museum is located on Skeppsholmen, the tiny island just along from the Grand Hotel, which has great views looking over the water. One of the best ways to enjoy the museum is to come for the excellent weekend brunch at the Grand before exploring the collection. (Reservations necessary).

National Museum, Södra Blasieholmshamnen, Östermalm

Tel: 08 5195 4300 www.nationalmuseum.se
Open: 11am–5pm (8pm Tues, Thurs). Closed Mondays.

The largest art museum in Sweden has a remarkable collection housed in a building that's reminiscent of Florentine and Venetian Renaissance architecture. There are works by Rembrandt, Manet, Goya, Rubens, Renoir, Degas, Gauguin, and the most notable 18th- and 19th-century Swedish artists

(including John Tobias Sergel, Carl Larsson and Anders Zorn). There's a wealth of Scandinavian paintings and sculptures, dating back to the 16th century, as well as applied arts and modern design including the Gustavsberg Porcelain Collection. Pieces from the royal collections are regularly displayed and the museum hosts international touring exhibitions. During the summer months, guided tours are available in English, but it's more fun to work your way through the rooms on your own.

Nobel Museum, Stortorget, Gamla Stan

Tel: 08 5348 1800 www.nobelmuseum.se
Open: summer: daily, 10am–5pm (8pm Tues); winter: 11am–5pm (8pm Tues). Closed Mondays.

In this beautiful 18th-century building on the main square in Gamla Stan you can learn about the various Nobel laureates – Al Gore (Peace, 2007), Marie Curie (Chemistry, 1911), Winston Churchill (Literature, 1953), Mikhail Gorbachev (Peace, 1990), Guglielmo Marconi (Physics, 1909) and so forth. You can also find out more about Alfred Nobel, the Stockholmer who made

a fortune with the invention of dynamite and then bequeathed his wealth to establish the world's most prestigious prize. There are regular temporary exhibitions focusing on particular Nobel Laureates (such as, from 2007, 'Churchill: Painter and Writer'). Don't miss the autographs in the Café Satir: Nobel laureates are invited to sign the underside of the chairs. If you are in the city in October, it is possible to attend the announcements of some of the prizes (check www.nobelprize.org for details).

Nordiska Museet, Djurgårdsvagen 6–16, Djurgården
Tel: 08 5195 4600   www.nordiskamuseet.se
Open: 10am–6pm (8pm Weds) Mon–Fri; 11am–5pm Sat–Sun

The Nordiska Museet (Nordic Museum) is Sweden's biggest museum of cultural history and shows all the traditions and trends of Swedish life through

the centuries. It was created by Artur Hazelius, the man who was responsible for founding Skansen (see page 130). The Nordiska is located close to the Vasa Museum (see page 131), so you can cover both these treasures in one day. When you walk into the museum, the first thing you'll see is a gigantic statue of Gustav Vasa, who became King of Sweden in 1523. There are scores of exhibitions covering different aspects of Nordic life, everything from folk art and the Sami people who live in the far north to a history of table settings since the 16th century and rooms furnished in perfect 1950s mid-century modern style.

The Royal Palace, Gamla Stan

Tel: 08 402 6130 www.royalcourt.se
Open: daily, 10am–4pm mid-May–Aug; noon–3pm Tues–Sun Sep–mid-May

The imposing Royal Palace towers over the narrow streets of Gamla Stan. No one will ever accuse it of being the world's most beautiful palace, but it is one of the largest. The Royal Family no longer lives here from day to day

– they moved out to Drottningholm in 1981 – but it remains the monarch's official residence. You can visit the opulent royal apartments, the royal chapel or one of several museums housed in the building. Or just stop by to see the changing of the guards, which takes place every day at noon. In the Livrustkammaren (Royal Armoury) underneath the palace you can see the outfit King Gustav III was wearing when he was murdered at a masked ball in 1792, an event that inspired Verdi's opera *Un Ballo in Maschera*.

Skansen, Djurgårdsslätten 49, Djurgården

Tel: 08 442 8000   www.skansen.se

Open every day of the year; times vary so check the website for details

Skansen covers several acres of Djurgården and attracts more than a million visitors every year – and deservedly so. It appeals to everyone by combining

an open-air museum featuring 160 historic buildings from the 18th, 19th and 20th centuries with an extensive zoo. You can see elk, lynx, brown bears, seals, reindeer and owls, or visit the aquarium. Watching the wolves being fed is always particularly popular. Alternatively take a ride on the funicular railway then head over to the picnic pavilion, rose garden, herb garden or the farm. It's a mark of just how good Skansen is that it's one of the few museums in the city

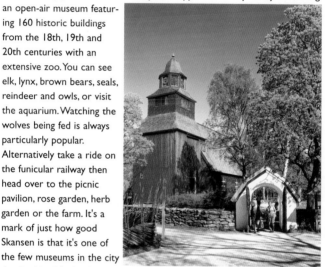

that is visited by locals, as well as visitors. Each year it hosts Allsång på Skansen, an old-fashioned sing-along concert, which is hugely popular with Swedes – and baffling to everyone else.

Thielska Galleriet, Sjötullsbacken 8, Djurgården

Tel: 08 662 5884   www.thielska-galleriet.se

Open: daily, noon (1pm Sun)–4pm

This beautiful Art Nouveau building is off the main tourist track but well worth discovering. If it were any closer to the centre it would undoubtedly be permanently mobbed. The Thielska was completed in 1907, and was built as a private home designed to showcase the art collection of a successful banker, Ernest Thiel. Thiel was personal friends with many notable Scandinavian artists and as a result the collection includes many works by

Carl Larsson, an enormously popular Swedish artist, and several pieces by the Norwegian Edvard Munch of *The Scream* fame. The building is located at the far end of Djurgården, the opposite end to the Vasa Museet, so to reach it you can either take a pleasantly long stroll or alternatively just jump onto the number 69 bus, which runs from Kungsholmen via Norrmalm and takes you almost to the door of the gallery.

Vasamuseet, Galärvarvsvägen 14, Djurgården.

Tel: 08 5195 4800 www.vasamuseet.se

Open: 10am–5pm daily (until 8pm Weds)

If you only visit one museum on your trip to Stockholm, visit the Vasa. It's unique, it's fascinating – and it's utterly stunning. The warship *Vasa* sank in

Stockholm harbour in 1628, moments after being launched for the first time. Its wreck was discovered in the 1950s and carefully salvaged. Despite being underwater for centuries it was in

remarkable condition. This is because the Great Shipworm, a hungry little mollusc that nibbles away most wooden wrecks, doesn't like the low-salt waters of the Baltic. The experience of seeing the ship is enhanced by the intelligent design of the museum that surrounds it. It manages to bring the boat to life in a way that is fascinating for both children and adults. It's a good idea to start your visit by watching the film (which has English subtitles) which is shown in the auditorium near the entrance. Understanding how the ship was rediscovered and salvaged makes you appreciate just how extraordinary this museum is.

OPERA/THEATRE

Royal Opera House, Gustav Adolfs torg, Norrmalm
Tel: 08 791 4400 www.operan.se

The Royal Opera and the Royal Ballet make their home in this imposing building just across the water from the Royal Palace. The Opera House is more than just one of the cultural hearts of the city. It also has several excellent places to eat, drink and even spend the evening clubbing (see Operahuset, Eat, and Café Opera, Party). Each season brings a busy programme of ballet and opera. There are also regular guided tours of the building in English, which allow you to go backstage and see the King and Queen's private suite. Performances range from the expected classics to more modern productions, such as *Pippi Longstocking: The Ballet*, during which a pair of enormous ginger pigtails was attached to the roof of the building. Visit the website for full details and to buy tickets.

Dramaten, Nybroplan, Östermalm
Tel: 08 667 06 80 www.dramaten.se

Kungliga Dramatiska Teatern, commonly known as Dramaten, is Sweden's National Theatre. It occupies a beautiful white marble building dating from 1908 on Nybroplan, and is built in Jugendstil, the Scandinavian version of Art Nouveau. This is the theatre that was, for many years, the artistic home of Ingmar Bergman (he was the theatre's director 1960–66, and its manager 1963-66) while alumni from the acting school include Greta Garbo and Max von Sydow (the actor who played chess with Death in Bergman's *The Seventh Seal*). These days productions range from the classics to contemporary Swedish and foreign dramas, including plays for children, though most performances are, of course, in Swedish. Occasionally there are also concerts here (Rufus Wainwright played several nights in 2008). Outside the building you'll see a life-sized bronze statue of Margaretha Krook, who was one of Sweden's greatest actresses. Feel free to pat her tummy – she is Stockholm's only heated statue.

CINEMA

You'll have no problem finding a cinema in Stockholm, ranging from huge multi-screen complexes to smaller, more charming venues showing alternative films. With the exception of children's films, English-language movies are never dubbed into Swedish but are instead subtitled. Full listings can be found in *Dagens Nyheter*, *Svenska Dagbladet* or the free newspapers that are handed out on the underground.

Filmstaden Sergel, Hötorget, Norrmalm
Tel: 08 5626 0000 www.sf.se

A massive multiplex, located on the square at Hörtorget, where the major releases get their debut. Best avoided if you are allergic to chattering Swedish teenagers or the overpowering smell of popcorn.

Grand, Sveavägen 45, Vasastan
Tel: 08 5626 0000

Arguably the loveliest of Stockholm's cinemas, and one of the most comfortable, with an excellent range of films. It is the cinema from which Prime Minister Olof Palme was walking home when he was murdered in 1986.

Rigoletto, Kungsgatan 16, Norrmalm
Tel: 08 5626 0000 www.sf.se

A large, popular multiplex a short walk from Stureplan that shows everything from the newest blockbusters to obscure art movies.

Zita, Birger Jarlsgatan 37, Östermalm
Tel: 08 23 20 20 www.zita.se

The Zita has a reputation for being one of the more alternative cinemas in town, regularly showing films you won't find elsewhere.

TICKETS

For the many theatres, concerts and sporting events, tickets can be booked online from Ticnet (www.ticnet.se), which has an English language site. There's also a ticket office conveniently located in the middle of Norrmalmstorg, close to NK. There's rarely too much of a queue and you can often pick up some last-minute tickets here.

shop...

No one will ever accuse Stockholm of being a bargain hunter's paradise. But if you are motivated more by a sense of style than a love of thrift, it's a great shopping city.

Upon arriving in the town, most tourists make a beeline for Gamla Stan. As a result, the Old Town is blighted with far too many shops that specialize in such tasteful items as moose-shaped fridge magnets and T-shirts with lewd slogans about Vikings. However, if you look around you'll find that there are also a handful of shops selling high-quality Swedish glass from Kosta Boda and Orrefors and some of the better sorts of crafts, so it is possible to find something nice to take away with you.

A far more sensible starting point for anyone new to Stockholm would be to head straight to NK. Nordiska Kompaniet, to give it its full title (which no one uses), is the most elegant department store in town. You can happily spend hours here familiarizing yourself with Scandinavian tastes in everything from kitchen products to cocktail dresses. Afterwards, the revolving clock and neon sign on NK's roof serves as a useful landmark as you begin to navigate the streets around it.

NK stands on Hamngatan, which is home to several other Swedish shops, including H&M for super-affordable fashion, and Polarn o Pyret for baby clothes. It's also close to three of the city's busiest shopping streets: Birger Jarlsgatan, Biblioteksgatan and Drottninggatan.

Birger Jarlsgatan and Biblioteksgatan are both known for their designer-label boutiques (though the former is posher than the latter). Drottninggatan, on the other hand, caters more to the other end of the shopping spectrum. It's pedestrianized and always packed, and is best avoided. Rather like London's Oxford Street, it's largely shabby, always exhausting and rarely inspiring.

Other parts of town offer a variety of shopping experiences. Östermalm, the most exclusive quarter, continues the focus on high-end fashion and design. You'll find most of the major domestic and international labels represented. It is home to Svenskt Tenn, the country's most famous interior décor store.

Kungsholmen has the Västermalmsgallerian, a small shopping mall with brands including Björn Borg (yes, that Björn Borg, whose name is now used on a range of sporty clothes and underwear), FACE Stockholm cosmetics and a small

H&M. Nearby is R.O.O.M., which is like a Swedish version of the Conran Shop. It's good to visit it for ideas as well as the excellent range of furniture and other items for sale.

For more alternative, bohemian shops and small independent labels that more accurately reflect the street fashions of Stockholm, head over to Södermalm and explore along and around Götgatan, Skånegatan and Åsögatan. In a cunning bit of marketing, the area south of Folkungagatan has been branded as SoFo, echoing the way in which the area south of Houston Street in New York is known as SoHo, though the shopping on offer in this neighbourhood is much more modest.

R.O.O.M., Alströmergatan 20

While Svenskt Tenn is the place for a more classic Swedish style, R.O.O.M. is a huge place that sells much more modern furnishings. It's not all Nordic; they also have an excellent collection of English wallpapers. It's far from cheap but even if you don't want to shop for that perfect Scandinavian sofa it's worth visiting to get ideas and be inspired by the pieces on display. A walk over to R.O.O.M. is a popular weekend stroll for lots of locals.

Västermalmsgallerian, St Eriksgatan 45

This compact shopping mall helped to pioneer the revival of the Fridhemsplan area of Kungsholmen. You enter past the Dubbel-W café, which is always busy, and a popular Apple computer store. Shops include MQ, Björn Borg and Solo for clothes, Granit for cool household items, and high-quality Swedish cosmetics at FACE Stockholm.

Acne, Norrmalmstorg 2

The most fashionable denim brand in town. Even if you are not looking to buy some of their jeans, it's worth popping in to the store on Norrmalmstorg as it's of historical significance. It was here, in 1973, that a bank robbery led to a hostage situation that in turn gave rise to the phrase 'Stockholm syndrome'. Today the bank's vaults are the shop's storeroom. Apparently, sometimes criminals return to the scene of their crime – the staff report that one of the bank robbers came in once to see how it had changed.

Åhléns, Klarabergsgatan 50

This mid-range department store has an excellent collection of clothes, both Scandinavian and international, as well as glass, china, homewares and cosmetics, and a great music department. You can have a facial or a massage in the Åhléns Day Spa on the top floor or buy groceries on the lower level in the Hemköp grocery store.

Gallerian, Hamngatan 37

One of the first malls in Stockholm, Gallerian had a much-needed facelift a few years ago and has seemed much busier and brighter ever since. It's a mass-market sort of place where you'll find Topshop, Benetton, The Phonehouse, Body Shop, Puma and Levi's. Just the sort of place, in other words, that attracts hordes of teenagers at the weekend. There are a dozen or so places to eat or drink, ranging from the Espresso House to sushi bars.

Hamngatan

Hamngatan is home to NK and also the place where you'll find Swedish megabrand H&M, as well as its big rival, Zara. There's also Polarn o Pyret, a children's clothing store known for its stripy fabrics which you'll see on babies all over the country. The kiddie clothes aren't cheap, but parents love their durability.

Hötorget

Stockholm's main outdoor market sells fresh fruit and flowers Monday–Saturday and then hosts a (not particularly good) flea market on Sundays. Whenever you walk through the market the stallholders shout out their bargains to get your attention, which some people find charming and others find irritating. Don't miss the indoor market, Hötorgetshallen, which is located underneath the cinema complex. It's great for international foods and has lots of places where you can perch at a counter for a quick snack.

NK, Hamngatan 18–20

The crown jewel of Stockholm shopping. A sort of Scandinavian Selfridges (or Baltic Barneys), packed with excellent boutiques. NK is particularly good for clothes shopping, but there's an extensive glass and kitchenware department downstairs and, on the top floor, one of the best English bookshops in town. Café Entré in the main entrance is always popular, but there are also more cafés downstairs near the grocery department.

PUB, Hötorget

PUB (named after its founder, Paul U. Bergström) is most famous for being the department store that once employed a young Stockholm girl called Greta Garbo to model hats. But that was a long time ago, and of late it has become the poor relation of the city's other more dominating department stores. A baffling interior layout hardly helps. It's currently undergoing a major renovation which must, surely, restore some of its lost glamour.

ÖSTERMALM

Biblioteksgatan

Located just off Stureplan, Biblioteksgatan is known for its many clothes stores and shoe shops, including Emporio Armani, Rizzo, Geox, Karen Millen, Mathilde, Kookai, Peak Performance and, in a converted cinema, Urban Outfitters. There are also several jewellers and high-end watch shops.

Birger Jarlsgatan

This is the place for big labels with high prices. There's Gucci (at number 1), Hugo Boss (24), Louis Vuitton (17), Max Mara (12), Versace (21) and many more. There's also modern Danish silver at George Jensen, antique Swedish silver at Kurt Ribbhagen, and Swedish crystal at Orrefors and Kosta Boda (all at number 13). Rönnells (32) sells antiquarian books while Efva Attling (9) and Thomas Szabo (15) are extremely fashionable contemporary jewellers.

Grev Turegatan

Here you'll find one of the best branches of Filippa K, the clothing store for men and women that is almost like a uniform for professional Stockholmers, as well as Ease, Filippa's spin-off store that sells super-casual womenswear. There's also J. Lindeberg, whose belts can be seen around so many Swedish hips, La Chemise, which is great for shirts, and Danish fashion brand Bruuns Bazaar. The various cafés with outdoor seating provide prime people-watching in the summer.

Modernity, Sibyllegatan 6

The best store in the city for mid-century modern furniture, ceramics and glass. Most of the pieces are Scandinavian. Prices are high but so is the level of service and quality. A must-visit shop for anyone with an interest in 20th-century Scandinavian design.

Saluhallen, Östermalmstorg

This unmissable 19th-century food hall is packed with meat, fish, vegetables, chocolate, bread and many more of life's essentials. There are also several places to eat lunch, including Lisa Elmqvist and Gerdas (see page 104) for memorable seafood. Whether dining or shopping, it's a great experience and one of the city's treasures, though it can be jam-packed around noon. Go a little later to avoid the main lunchtime rush.

Sturegallerien, Stureplan

The poshest mall in town links Stureplan with Grev Turegatan. Here you can browse Hedengrens bookshop, which has an extensive English language section, pause for cake at Gateau, and pick up some things at Fred Perry, Kenzo, Björn Borg and J. Lindeberg.

Svenskt Tenn, Strandvägen 5

The most famous interiors store in the land, Svenskt Tenn (the name means 'Swedish Pewter', which is what it originally specialized in) is best-known for the range of bold, beautiful, instantly recognizable fabrics by Josef Frank. The store's founder, Estrid Ericson, had a profound impact on the direction of Swedish decorating not least with her fondness for plain white walls.

SÖDERMALM

Götgatan

This is one of the trendier places to shop in Stockholm. Here you'll find younger fashions at stores like Weekday. There's also a mini-mall called Bruno Götgatsbacken, which houses Adidas, American Apparel, Reiss, Whyred, Filippa K and more.

play...

Swedes love being outside. The ability to sail, ski and skate is considered just about as important as reading, writing and arithmetic.

The country has one of the highest rates of boat ownership in the world. Similarly, having a second home isn't limited to the wealthy. It's quite common for families of far more modest means to have a place in the country, often just a simple wooden house painted red or yellow. It may not even be winter-proofed but it provides a summertime escape.

Unlike some other nationalities, when they have a bank holiday – known in Sweden as a red day because they're printed in diaries in red ink – Stockholmers much prefer to leave the city than race to the shops. Anyone visiting the city in July might notice that the capital has a certain ghost town quality to it, with streets half-empty and many businesses closed. That's because July is the national holiday, and many of the residents decamp to the land.

Perhaps this is all a result of having such a challenging winter. When the warm days of summer come around the Swedes know they have to make the most of them. One of Stockholm's greatest charms is the ease with which you can swap concrete for country-side, whether by car or by boat. Sailing around the thousands of islands that make up Stockholm's archi-pelago on a sunny day is sublime. There are many ferries that you can take out to the archipelago, and various lodging

options ranging from hotels to simple cabins and campsites, but the best way to explore it is on a private boat. After sailing for a few hours you moor at some uninhabited island and make lunch, boiling the potatoes in a pan of Baltic seawater.

If you do remain in the city, there are acres of parkland to be enjoyed. There's Haga Park, just north of Vasastan, and Djurgården, the greenest of the central islands. You'll feel as if you're out in the middle of the Swedish countryside even though you are just minutes from the heart of the city. You can easily go swimming in the clean water surrounding Kungsholmen or Långholmen.

While the onset of winter is always grim, a midwinter snowfall can be magical. If it gets cold enough, the waters around the city freeze solid and people promptly start walking, skiing and skating on them, undeterred by the occasional news reports of people sent to their doom when the ice breaks beneath them. A good rule for visitors is to watch what the locals do – if they're taking short-cuts by walking on the ice, feel free to do the same, but if they're staying on land, you would be wise to follow suit.

At any time of year there are also spas, both in the city and just outside it, where you can experience a Swedish massage at first hand. For more information on activities, visit Stockholm's official visitors' website: www.stockholm-town.com

Stockholm's size, beauty and numerous parks and cycle lanes mean that biking is a great way to spend some time and get a feel for the city. Bikes can be hired at reasonable prices. In 2007, the City Bike system was introduced. During the warmer months people can borrow from a fleet of blue-and-white bikes that can be taken from stands located around town and used for up to three hours. You need a membership card, but a day-card costs an incredibly low 25kr. For more information visit: www.stockholmcitybikes.se

Cykel och Moped Uthyrningen, Kajplats 24 Strandvägen, Östermalm
Tel: 08 660 7959   www.rentabike.se
Open: daily, 10am–6pm

City bikes, mountain bikes and even tandems are available to rent for a relaxed trip around the city. Roller-blades and mopeds are also on offer.

Djurgårdsbrons Sjöcafé, Galärvarvsvägen 2, Djurgården
Tel: 08 660 5757
Open: daily, 10am–midnight

As well as hiring bikes you can also hire kayaks and canoes, or stop off for a coffee on the waterfront.

FOOTBALL

Football is the biggest spectator sport in the country, with Sven-Göran Eriksson (known in Sweden by the nickname Svennis) and Freddie Ljungberg just two of the big names. Fans have been rewarded by Sweden's constant appearance at European and World cups, though Stockholm's three main teams, Hammarby, Djurgården and AIK, haven't had much success in European club football in recent years. The city has several major stadiums, and there are many matches to choose from. As you might expect, Swedish domestic football takes a prolonged break through the winter months.

AIK, Råsunda Fotbollstadion, Solnavägen 51, Solna
www.aik.se

With a capacity of 37,000, Råsunda is one of the largest stadiums in the country. Home to AIK, it hosts occasional UEFA cup ties.

Hammarby, Söderstadion, Arenavägen
Tel: 08 725 1243 www.hammarbyfotboll.se

Far smaller, this stadium is on a par with some of the UK's Third Division clubs, holding a mere 11,100. However, Hammarby competes in the A League, where they put up a good fight against the likes of Malmö and Göteborg.

Globen, Arenavägen, Johaneshov
Tel: 08 600 3400; Box Office: 077 131 00 00 www.globen.se

Globen is the enormous spherical venue that can be seen rising like the moon on the city's southern skyline. It is the likely venue for many major sporting events as well as concerts.

For tickets to any of the games, contact the clubs direct, or use a local ticket agency: Biljett Direkt, Tel: 0771 70 70 70 www.biljett.se, one of the biggest ticket brokers in Stockholm.

GOLF

With Swedish golfers Fredrik Jacobson and Annika Sorenstam making a huge impact on the golfing world, the sport is inevitably acquiring an intense following. There are at least 50 golf courses within easy reach of Stockholm's city centre, some more immediately accessible than others. For information visit www.sgf.golf.se or book yourself in at one of the following:

Djursholms Golfklubb, Hagbardsvägen 1, Djursholm
Tel: 08 5449 6451 www.dgk.nu

Beautifully set and the closest to the city centre, with green fees starting at 350kr (150kr for juniors).

Kungsängens Golf Club, Garpebodavägen 1, Kungsangen
Tel: 08 5845 0730   www.kungsangengc.se
Open: 9am–2pm Mon–Fri

A serious course for serious golfers, this club has hosted the Scandinavian Masters four times.

Wermdö, Torpa, Värmdö
Tel: 08 5746 0720   www.wgcc.nu
Open: 9am–4pm Mon–Fri

This beautiful course in the countryside 18 miles (30 km) outside Stockholm is well worth the trip

ICE HOCKEY

Fans support their ice hockey teams with gusto during the winter. So much so, in fact, that as a spectator sport it's nearly as popular as football. And, as with football, the major teams are Hammarby, AIK and Djurgården. For tickets and info visit the team's website or Globen, where the major teams play regularly.

AIK
Tel: 08 735 9600   www.aik.se

Djurgården
Tel: 08 5561 0800   www.difhockey.se

Hammarby
Tel: 08 462 8825   www.hammarby-if.se

Swedes love sailing and love skating, so it's only naturally that they're also enthusiastic ice sailors. The Swedish Ice Sailing Federation includes around 50 local clubs and their website has maps and other information: www.issegling.se.

Several outdoor skating rinks appear each winter in the city, but there are also year-round places to skate indoors. However, if it gets cold enough the waters around Stockholm will freeze. Skating lanes and even coffee stands appear on the ice. Suddenly you can take short cuts between islands by walking across the frozen water. In a good, cold winter, it's possible to take skating trips around the archipelago or head inland on Lake Mälaren. Each year (weather allowing) there is a famous skating race, the Vikingarännet, which covers 80 kilometres (50 miles) between Stockholm and Uppsala. It usually takes place in February. It attracts around 4,000 participants. You can learn more and sign up for the race at the website: www.vikingarannet.com

Kungsträdgården, Östermalm
Tel: 08 789 2490

This outdoor rink is set up each winter and is most fun at night when you skate under floodlights. Popular with children. Skate hire is available for 30kr. Call the Swedish tourist office for further details.

Medborgplatsen, Södermalm
Tel: 08 789 2490

Outdoors and tiny, this is mostly full of families and amateur skaters, as there isn't much room for the more adventurous. Skates are reasonably priced. Winter only.

Stockholms Skridskoseglarklubb
(The Stockholm Ice Skate Sailing and Touring Club)
www.sssk.se

This website has an introduction in English to ice skating in the Stockholm area.

Zinkensdamms Idrottplats, Ringvägen 12–14, Södermalm
Tel: 08 668 9331

You'll find games going on here most of the day, which are fun to watch and, if you're feeling brave, you can take part. It's open all year and the admission is free.

SAILING

Swedes have one of the highest rates of boat ownership in the world, and during the summer an armada of private yachts heads out from the city and into the archipelago. Many keen sailors head for Sandhamn, an island in the archipelago that's a popular stopping-off point for yachts. Each summer there's a famous boat race, the Gotland Runt, organized by the Royal Swedish Yacht Club, which goes out of Sandhamn and around the Baltic island of Gotland.

Kungliga Svenska Segel Sällskapet (The Royal Swedish Yacht Club)
Tel: 08 5561 6680 www.ksss.se

Although the website is in Swedish it has many links (*länkar*) to other sites, including one devoted to the Gotland Runt, which have English content.

Classic Yacht Chater, Karlbergs Strand 4, Solna
Tel: 08 5875 5740 www.classicyachtcharter.se

From modern motor yachts to classic steamboats, Classic Yacht Charter offers a range of trips and options around Stockholm and throughout Sweden.

Stockholm Yacht Charter, Vikingavägen 17 B, Saltsjöbaden
Tel: 08 5716 7130 www.sycharter.com

Stockholm Yacht Charter offers a selection of motor cruisers and yachts, and trips around the archipelago lasting from a day to a week.

SKIING

If you're a serious skier then you'll have to venture a way out of the city for anything resembling an Alpine slope. However, for a day's amusement, beginning in some cases with a long, early morning bus ride, decent snow at the right time of year isn't a million miles away. Reliable information is available at www.skiinfo.se.

Flottsbro, TomtbergaHuge Fastigheter, 141 22 Huddinge
Tel: 08 5353 2700 www.flottsbro.com

Located 40km south of the city and intended for the unambitious skier, since the runs are fairly tame. Don't make this more than a day trip.

Hammarbybacken, Hammarby Fabriksväg 90, Hammarby
Tel: 08 641 8540 www.skistar.se

This man-made slope just south of Södermalm is easily accessible from the city. It has great views over the town and surrounding area, and you can easily spend some time exploring the small but fascinating town of Hammarby Sjöstad.

Kungsberget
Tel: 02 9076 7300 www.kungsberget.se

Great for the avid snowboarder, this resort features an impressive half-pipe. To get here you should arrive in Stockholm before the weekend, since the bus leaves at 7am on Saturdays and Sundays to give you time for about 6 hours of snow action.

Centralbadet, Drottninggatan 88

Tel: 08 5452 1300   www.centralbadet.se

Open: 6am–8pm Mon–Fri; 8am–10pm Sat; 8am–5pm Sun

Although it's right on Drottninggatan, one of Stockholm's busiest shopping streets, it's easy to walk past the entrance to Centralbadet and not see it. It's set back from the street, behind a small garden area. Inside, it offers a range of treatments in a wonderfully old-fashioned building. The swimming pool is an Art Nouveau gem, complete with artificial seagulls overhead.

Skepparholmen, Franckes väg, Saltsjö-Boo

Tel: 08 747 6500   www.skepparholmen.se

Open: 9am–7pm Fri–Sat; 9am–5pm Sun

Set inside a large houseboat with wooden decks to sit out on in summer, Skepparholmen is within 20 minutes of Stockholm's hustle and bustle. It's a useful countryside retreat even if the spa doesn't interest you, but the spa is what made its name and the facilities are more carefully designed than the hotel itself. It focuses on comfort. Pad around in towelling flip-flops and a robe for a day or weekend, and then retire to enjoy the spectacular views from your room. Facilities include a swimming pool and gym, but the real treats are the treatments and massages.

Sturebadet, Sturegallerian 36, Östermalm

Tel: 08 5450 1500   www.sturebadet.se

Open: 6.30am–10pm Mon–Fri; 9am–7pm Sat–Sun

Stockholm's most celebrated spa, with a restaurant so good that it even attracts those not interested in the facilities and a list of treatments that never ends. It's also perfect for the flying visitor, since you needn't be a member to book a same-day appointment. Drop in for a traditional Swedish massage and relax in a Moroccan-inspired setting. The pool area is decorated with light-blue tiles and is the focal point of the spa.

Yasuragi, Hasseludden, Hamndalsvägen 6, Saltsjö-Boo

Tel: 08 747 6400 www.hasseludden.com

Functioning as a hotel and conference centre as well as spa, it is hard to know whether to visit Yasuragi for a day or week. As your taxi pulls up to this countryside retreat 15 minutes outside the city centre, don't be disheartened by an uninspiring exterior. Inside, the décor adheres faithfully to its Japanese theme, from the teppanyaki restaurant to minimalist bedrooms, with rattan mats on spacious, uncluttered floors and futons. It's worth spending a weekend here to reap the full benefits, but if a day is all you can spare, you'll still get something special out of it. The food, although intended to be healthy, is so delicious you won't be able to stop eating (which may slightly defeat your original purpose). However, treatments are definitely less luxurious than those of Sturebadet – they want you to feel cleansed and detoxed by the end, rather than more beautiful. If you have time, try one of the yoga or meditation lessons.

SWIMMING

Eriksdalsbadet, Hammarby Slussväg 20, Södermalm

Tel: 08 5084 0250 www.eriksdalsbadet.com

Open: 6.30am–9pm (8pm Fri) Mon–Fri; 9am–5pm Sat; 9am–6pm Sun

Of course, in the summertime all you need to do is grab a towel and head down to Långholmen or Norr Mälarstrand for a splash. But when it's too cold, or if you want to do laps, head to Eriksdalsbadet. Located on the southern edge of Södermalm, beside the Clarion hotel, it has two large pools for serious swimmers, plus a great play area with slides, tunnels and even a submerged entrance to an outside pool you swim to even in the dead of winter. For anyone with children, it's a perfect place. Day admission: Adult 75kr; 4–19 years old 35kr, family ticket (1–2 children, 2 adults) 185kr.

Outdoor tennis courts are available for much of the year, and there are also indoor courts for those keen to play all year round.

Haga Tennis, Haga Kungspark, Solna
Tel: 08 33 7077   www.hagatennis.se
Open: check website for times, which vary throughout the year

These courts are set in charming scenery in the middle of Haga Park. Courts cost from 100kr an hour.

Kungliga Tennishallen, Lidingövägen 75, Hjorthagen
Tel: 08 459 1500   www.kltk.se
Open: 6.45am–11pm Mon–Thurs; 6.45am–10pm Fri; 7.45am–8.30pm Sat; 8.45am–10.30 Sun

The Royal Lawn Tennis Club of Stockholm is known for hosting the Stockholm Open ATP tournament every year. A court costs about 250kr an hour.

Tennisstadion, Fiskartorpsvägen 20, Stockholm
Tel: 08 5452 5254
Open: 7am–11pm Mon–Thurs; 7am–10pm Fri; 8am–9pm Sat; 8am–10pm Sun

With indoor and outdoor courts, this tennis centre just north of Öster-malm is a great place year-round. Rackets and balls cost extra to hire on top of the court charge, which starts at 260kr for an hour.

Notes & Updates

info...

DANGERS

Stockholm is, by and large, an extremely safe city. Common sense – watching out for pickpockets, being alert when strolling the city late at night – should be all that's necessary to ensure a crime-free visit.

LANGUAGE

Not only do virtually all Swedes speak English, they speak it fluently and gladly. Of course, it's only good manners that you should learn a few words of Swedish for your visit (at the very least, say '*tack*' for thank you), but if you try to be any more ambitious you may run into problems. It's a quirk of Swedish that if you mispronounce a word even slightly, Swedes find it incredibly difficult to understand what you are saying. This can cause problems in cabs, so it's wise to have the address of your destination written down if it looks at all hard to say.

MONEY

At the time of writing, the Swedish kroner has a rough exchange rate as follows: £1 = 12kr; Euro1 = 9kr; US$1 = 6kr. It's far simpler to get money from cashpoints and banks than it is to take travellers' cheques or money to exchange. And absolutely everywhere, including taxis and bars, accepts credit cards.

PUBLIC TRANSPORT

Stockholm's tube system, the *tunnelbana*, is extremely simple to use. Directions are clear and the English-speaking staff helpful. Similarly, buses are pleasant and routes relatively easy to understand. The easiest way to get around is to buy a travel card or a '*remsa*', a strip of paper that the bus driver or underground ticket agent stamps. Once stamped, you can use it on any other bus or subway for one hour. The city has even introduced tickets that can be downloaded to your mobile phone, though more traditional ticketing methods are still more popular. Note that you will often see people – from unwashed teens to middle-aged office workers who should know better – brazenly climbing over the turnstiles to avoid paying. It is illegal, and if caught you will be fined. Tickets cost: single 20kr, 8-ride card 180kr, 1-day card 100kr, 3-day card 200kr, 7-day card 260kr.

info...

Boats can be useful to get around the city. The most popular ferry is the one that links Gamla Stan, Djurgården and Östermalm. The tourist office has full ferry timetables, as well as information on boat trips out to the archipelago.

STOCKHOLM CARD

The Stockholm Card gives unlimited free public transport on buses and the *tunnelbana*, plus access to 75 of the city's main attractions and some sightseeing boat tours. It can be bought from the tourist office (see below) or online at www.stockholmtown.com. Latest prices: 1-day Stockholm Card 330kr (child 160kr), 2-day Stockholm Card 460kr (child 190kr), 3-day Stockholm Card 580kr (child 220kr).

TOURIST OFFICE

The official tourist office is located on Hamngatan, roughly opposite NK. If you need information or want to buy the Stockholm Card, you can also visit their website: www.stockholmtown.com. Stockholm Tourist Centre, Hamngatan 27 (entrance from Kungsträdgården), Tel: 08 5082 8508 Open: 9am–7pm Mon–Fri, 10am–5pm Sat, 10am–4pm Sun. Closed 24 and 25 December and 1 January.

TAXIS

This isn't New York or London. In Stockholm, people don't stand on a street corners waving umbrellas and shouting 'Taxi!'. Instead, they just whip out their mobile phones. While you are, of course, allowed to hail them on the street, it's usually quicker and easier to telephone, particularly during busy periods. Once you've rung, taxis often appear with amazing speed, so start dialling only when you are ready to depart. Two words of warning: first, cabs are expensive. A short ride can easily cost over 100kr. Second, stick to the city's most reputable companies. Not only are they trustworthy but their cars are smoke-free and well kept, and the drivers know the city (and have GPS to help them if puzzled). Never get into one of the unmarked cars that you'll see doing illicit taxi work late at night.

Hg2 Stockholm

info...

Taxi Stockholm and Taxi Kurir are both reputable, with easy-to-remember numbers: Taxi Stockholm (Tel: 08 150 000) and Taxi Kurir (Tel: 08 300 000).

TELEPHONES

All the telephone numbers in this book are given with the Stockholm prefix 08. The international Swedish code is +46. If you are going to be here for a long time and intend to make local calls, it is worth buying a Swedish pay-as-you-go SIM.

TIPPING

In restaurants, tips of 5–10% are appreciated at dinner. However, there's no tradition of tipping at lunchtime. You are not obliged to tip bar staff, but if your change includes a few kronor, it's considered good form to leave them on the bar. With taxis, it's normal to round up the amount a little, though tipping is not compulsory.

FROM A TO Ö

Note that Swedish has three extra letters – å, ä, and ö – that do not exist in English. These are not just normal letters with accents over them. What's more, they come at the end of the alphabet so bear this in mind if you are trying to look something up or use the phone book.

index

Hg2 Stockholm

index

index